Foreword

CW00385542

Reading – Comprehension and Word Reading is a six-book series written to support the the programmes of study for reading at key stages one and two. The books give equal foc and word reading, and the different kinds of teaching and learning experiences needed

Titles in this series are:

- *Reading – Comprehension and Word Reading – Year 1*
- *Reading – Comprehension and Word Reading – Year 2*
- *Reading – Comprehension and Word Reading – Year 3*
- *Reading – Comprehension and Word Reading – Year 4*
- *Reading – Comprehension and Word Reading – Year 5*
- *Reading – Comprehension and Word Reading – Year 6*

Contents

Format of the Books

There are 18 six-page units of work within each book, and three formal summative assessment units, one located after every six units.

Each of the 18 units relates to a specific genre of fiction or non-fiction and follows the same format:

A table of **Curriculum Links** is provided, which lists the curriculum objectives covered by the text, comprehension and word reading pupil pages. An outcome is listed for each objective, to aid teacher assessment. Each objective has been allocated a code to aid identification. A table listing these codes and objectives can be found on page ix.

The **Definition of Terms** section includes an explanation of technical literary and grammatical terms. Generally, these terms are not covered in the glossary supplied with the programmes of study for English. They are provided as an aid for the teacher and not for pupils to learn, although teachers may wish to use the information to assist pupils to understand and complete specific activities.

Links to other Curriculum Areas lists any statutory or non-statutory content relating to other programmes of study. This section is omitted if no links are included.

Teacher Page 1

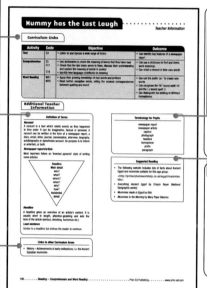

Terminology for Pupils is a list of technical literary and grammatical terms included in the unit. Pupils need to understand and use the terminology to complete the unit's activities.

Suggested Reading includes fiction and non-fiction books and/or digital material that relate to the content of the unit.

The **Notes and Guidance** provide detailed teaching points relating to each of the three pupil activity pages: text; comprehension; and word reading.

There are also summative assessment activities and answers.

The **Teacher Information** states the content of the copymaster activity and/or any materials the pupils may need.

The **Introduction** provides an activity for the class to complete before commencing the copymaster activity. It might involve a discussion, retelling the text in sequence or rereading the text in search of something specific.

Activities listed in the **Development** section might introduce or revise topics and/or suggest items to discuss, all with the aim of aiding pupils to work on the copymaster activity pages independently.

The **Differentiated Individual/Paired/Group Work** suggests differentiated additional activities related to the pupil activity pages.

The **Review** provides opportunities to discuss and/or share work to assess and conclude each activity.

Teacher Pages 2 and 3

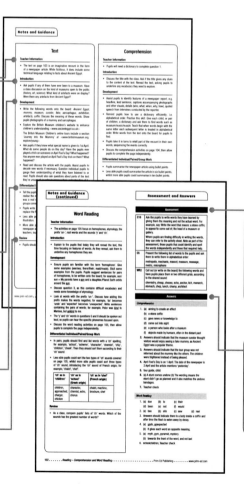

The **Assessment** table provides assessment activities for the pupil copymaster activity pages.

All the **Answers** are provided for the comprehension and word reading activity pages.

www.prim-ed.com

READING
COMPREHENSION AND WORD READING

YEAR 3

Lesson Plans, Texts, Comprehension Activities, Word Reading Activities and Assessments for the Year 3 English Curriculum.

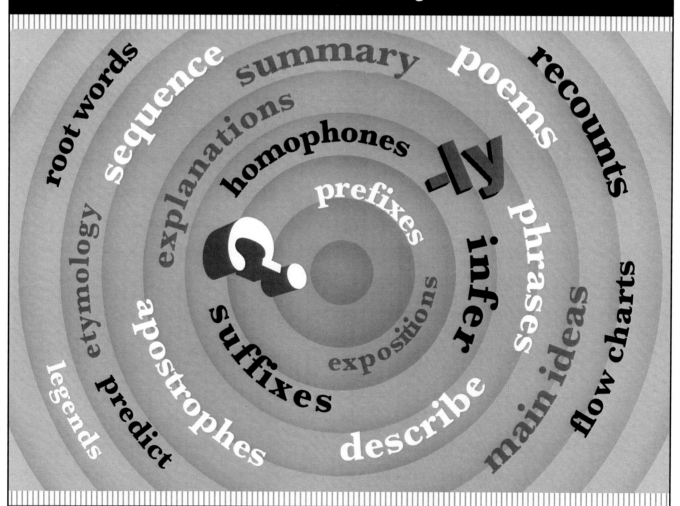

Monitor and track pupil progress with a FREE digital assessment tool.

COMPREHENSION

☑ Wide variety of text genres

☑ Activities to deepen comprehension

☑ Self-assessment for pupils

WORD READING

☑ Focus on word reading elements

☑ Activities to practise word reading skills

☑ Self-assessment for pupils

Reading – Comprehension and Word Reading (Year 3)

Published by Prim-Ed Publishing® 2015
Copyright© R.I.C. Publications® 2015

ISBN 978-1-84654-796-6

PR–2977

Titles available in this series:

Reading – Comprehension and Word Reading – *Year 1*
Reading – Comprehension and Word Reading – *Year 2*
Reading – Comprehension and Word Reading – *Year 3*
Reading – Comprehension and Word Reading – *Year 4*
Reading – Comprehension and Word Reading – *Year 5*
Reading – Comprehension and Word Reading – *Year 6*

Internet websites

In some cases, websites or specific URLs may be recommended. While these are checked and rechecked at the time of publication, the publisher has no control over any subsequent changes which may be made to webpages. It is *strongly* recommended that the class teacher checks *all* URLs before allowing pupils to access them.

View all pages online

Website: http://www.prim-ed.com

Email: sales@prim-ed.com

Format of the Books

Pupil Page 1

The **genre** of the fiction or non-fiction text the pupils are reading is provided. A list of the text genres is on page viii.

The **artwork** illustrates and supports the text.

The **Text focus** of the page is indicated.

Where possible, the **vocabulary in the texts** includes words from the spelling work and the spelling word list outlined in English Appendix 1 for each key stage.

The **learning log** provides an opportunity for pupils to self-assess their reading of the text.

Pupil Page 2

The **Comprehension focus** of the page is indicated.

Comprehension questions and activities relating to the text on *Pupil Page 1* are provided. The comprehension questions may relate to text structure or language features as well as text meaning.

The **answers** are provided on *Teacher Page 3*.

The **learning log** provides an opportunity for pupils to self-assess their completion of the activities.

Pupil Page 3

Word Reading questions and activities relating to the text on *Pupil Page 1* are provided. The main focus is the development of new vocabulary.

The **Word Reading focus** of the page is indicated. A list of the word reading concepts covered is on page viii.

The **answers** are provided on *Teacher Page 3*.

The **learning log** provides an opportunity for pupils to self-assess their completion of the activities.

Digital Assessment Tool

There is a digital assessment tool to accompany each book in the *Reading – Comprehension and Word Reading* series. This will enable teachers to monitor and track pupil progress. Teachers can download this assessment tool from the *Prim-Ed Publishing* website (www.prim-ed.com).

The home page of the download has the following features:

- Instructions for teachers;

- Quick-glance curriculum objectives and codes;

- Assessment by curriculum objectives; and

- Assessment by units in *Reading – Comprehension and Word Reading*.

Clicking the **Instructions for the teacher** icon provides an overview of the features of the download.

Clicking the **Quick-glance curriculum objectives and codes** icon shows the comprehension and word reading objectives from the curriculum and the codes that have been assigned to them in the book.

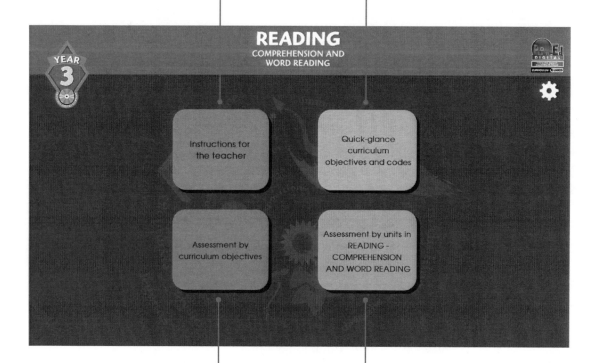

Clicking the **Assessment by curriculum objectives** icon displays each curriculum objective in a linear fashion, with advice and guidance to assess each one (more details are given on page vii).

Clicking the **Assessment by units in *Reading – Comprehension and Word Reading*** icon reveals an overview page allowing the teacher to click on the following options:

- Units (each individual unit in the book can be clicked);

- Formal Assessment (each of the three formal assessments can be clicked);

- Term (the three terms can be clicked); and

- End-of-Year (an overview of the pupil's yearly achievement).

Three categories and colour classifications of pupil progress are used throughout the assessment download. These categories are: working towards expectations (red), meeting expectations (orange) and exceeding expectations (green).

Teachers can assess by:

1. Curriculum objectives

- Click **Assessment by curriculum objectives** on the home page.

- Click on the code of the objective you are assessing. (Refer to the **Curriculum Objectives and Codes** on page xi, or click the quick-glance icon on the home page of the assessment tool and print them out.)

Type the pupils' names into the relevant column and save. This only has to be done once and the names will appear under every objective.

Record a description of the assessment used and the date of the assessment. Where applicable, the assessment activities in each unit of the book can be used to provide the evidence required to help teachers form an accurate picture of each pupil's progress. For example, page 10 presents an assessment activity based on the C1 objective and could be used as part of the evaluation.

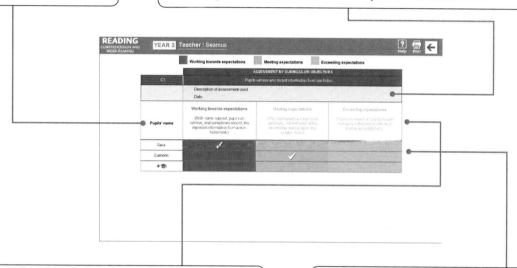

Read the advice and support under each category heading.

Click the box that best applies to each pupil's performance in relation to that objective.

To see a pupil's progress on the curriculum objectives that have been assessed to date, click the pupil's name and the following overview screen will be displayed:

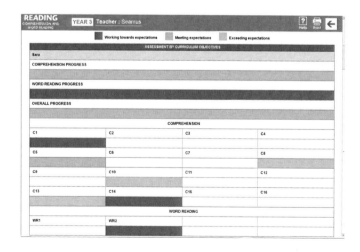

On this screen, which may be printed, the pupil's name is displayed. Progress in both comprehension and word reading are indicated by means of the appropriate colour. An overall progress colour is also displayed. Each curriculum code is displayed at the bottom of this page and the pupil's attainment in relation to this objective is indicated through the relevant colour. This allows teachers to see at a glance the objectives that require additional work.

Digital Assessment Tool ....

2. Units in *Reading – Comprehension and Word Reading*

- Click **Assessment by units in *Reading – Comprehension and Word Reading*** on the home page.

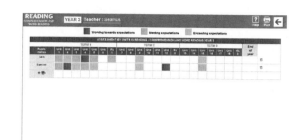

- Type in pupils' names.

    (a) Click on the required unit. For example, by clicking on **Unit 1** the codes of the objectives to be assessed in that unit will appear at the top.

    The pupils' names appear down the left-hand side. For each pupil, click the colour that best matches their achievement in relation to that objective. On returning to the page, an average score for that particular unit is displayed (as red, orange or green).

    (b) Click on **FA1**, **FA2** or **FA3**, once the pupils have completed the relevant formal assessment. The following screen will be displayed.

    Click each question the pupil got correct. A tick mark will be generated. Any questions that are not clicked (i.e. the incorrect ones) automatically receive an incorrect mark. The colour in the overall total bar at the base of the page indicates the pupil's performance.

    (c) Click on **TERM** at the end of each term. An end-of-term overview will be displayed, showing a performance colour for both comprehension and word reading.

    An overall average is also displayed, showing the combined progress in both comprehension and word reading. The results of the formal assessment for that term are also displayed on this screen. This screen can be printed for use in either pupil profile folders or parent-teacher meetings.

    (d) Click on **End-of-Year** at the end of the school year. This will display each pupil's overall progress for the entire school year. A breakdown of progress for each term is displayed, as well as progress in comprehension and word reading over the three terms. An overall average is also generated. This entire page can be printed out and passed on to the next teacher of this pupil.

Format of the Books

Three summative assessment units are included in each book, for pupils to take after every six units, or at the teacher's discretion.

The tests are based on the National Curriculum assessment guidelines.

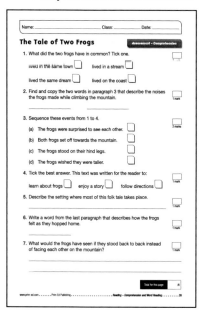

The **title** and **genre** of the text are given.

Artwork to illustrate and support the text.

Comprehension Assessment

Word Reading Assessment

Each question is awarded a mark to a total of 20 marks across the two pages. Inferential questions and multi-part questions are awarded a higher mark than literal questions. Pupils' scores can be recorded on the **Pupil Record Sheet** on page x.

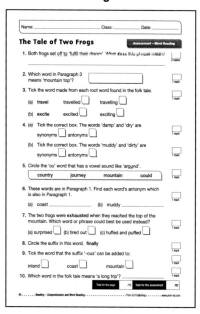

A **Teacher Information** page is provided to accompany each assessment unit.

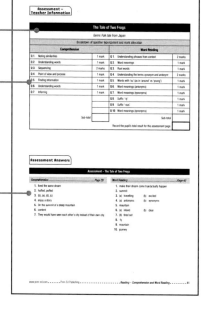

The **title** and **genre** of the text are given.

The **breakdown of question type/content** and the **mark allocation** are provided in a table. Teachers might choose to photocopy this table for each pupil, ticking/circling the questions answered correctly and recording the marks gained in each assessment and overall.

Answers are provided. Some questions are open-ended and will need to be teacher checked.

Text Genres

Unit	Fiction or Non-fiction?	Genre
1. Lazy Jack	fiction	fairy tale
2. How are Donkeys Different?	non-fiction	explanation
3. The Wise Old Donkey	fiction	folk tale
4. The Three Sillies	fiction	fairy tale
5. Wonderful Wales and Spectacular Scotland	non-fiction	retrieval chart/table
6. Wonderful Welsh Cakes	non-fiction	recipe
7. Ferocious Dragons	fiction	poem
8. Life Cycle of a Sunflower	non-fiction	explanation/flow chart
9. Yellow is the Best Colour	non-fiction	exposition
10. Stone Soup and Nail Soup	fiction	folk tale
11. The Stone Age	non-fiction	report
12. A Day at Skara Brae	non-fiction	diary
13. The Legend of Tam O'Shanter	fiction	legend
14. What's Going to Happen to Us?	fiction	play
15. Mummy Makers	non-fiction	report/procedure
16. Mummy has the Last Laugh	fiction	newspaper report
17. Fossil Poetry	fiction	poem
18. Types of Rocks	non-fiction	retrieval chart/table

Word Reading Concepts

Unit 1:	Lazy Jack	word meanings	synonyms	antonyms	root words
Unit 2:	How are Donkeys Different?	dictionary work	synonyms	homophones	suffix '-ous'
Unit 3:	The Wise Old Donkey	synonyms	root words	prefix 'dis-'	
Unit 4:	The Three Sillies	homophones	suffix '-ion'	'ou' sound (*young*)	'ou' sound (*around*)
Unit 5:	Wonderful Wales and Spectacular Scotland	prefix 'kilo-'	suffixes '-al' and '-ous'	antonyms/synonyms	'k' sound (*kitten*)
Unit 6:	Wonderful Welsh Cakes	root words	suffix '-ly'	adjectives and adverbs	nationalities
Unit 7:	Ferocious Dragons	syllables	words ending in '-ture'	synonyms	homophones and near-homophones
Unit 8:	Life Cycle of a Sunflower	words ending in '-sure'	words ending in '-tion'	synonyms	
Unit 9:	Yellow is the Best Colour	root words	the /s/ sound spelt 'sc'	word meanings	
Unit 10:	Stone Soup and Nail Soup	suffixes (-ly, -er, -ed, -ing, -ful)	antonyms	using prefixes 'un-', 'dis-' and 'mis-' to form opposites	
Unit 11:	The Stone Age	word categories	suffixes (-ly, -en, -er, -ed, -ing, -tion)	suffixes (doubling the final consonant when adding suffixes; e.g. *forgetting*)	homonyms: *rock* (noun/verb) and *skin* (noun/verb)
Unit 12:	A Day at Skara Brae	synonyms	antonyms	root words	words with the /ʃ/ sound spelt 'ch'
Unit 13:	The Legend of Tam O'Shanter	collective nouns	suffixes (-ly, -al, -able, -ed, -ing)	similes	homophones
Unit 14:	What's Going to Happen to Us?	prefix 're-'	root words	homophones	prefixes 'un-', 'dis-' and 'mis-'
Unit 15:	Mummy Makers	/s/ sound spelt 'sc'	synonyms and antonyms	suffixes (-y, -ing, -ed, -fully, -ation)	homophones
Unit 16:	Mummy has the Last Laugh	homophones	prefix 'un-'	/ɪ/ sound spelt 'y'	'ch' words
Unit 17:	Fossil Poetry	root words	prefix 'un-'	synonyms and antonyms	suffix '-sure'
Unit 18:	Types of Rocks	homophones	root words	synonyms	antonyms

Curriculum Objectives and Codes · · · · · · · · · · ·

The following table shows the word reading and comprehension objectives from the reading domain of the English programmes of study. Each objective has been assigned a code. These codes are used throughout the book to assist teachers in planning their work. They are also used in the **Curriculum Links** and **Assessment** tables of the **Teacher Pages**.

Word Reading

WR1	Pupils apply their growing knowledge of root words, prefixes and suffixes (etymology and morphology) as listed in English Appendix 1, both to read aloud and to understand the meaning of new words they meet.
WR2	Pupils read further exception words, noting the unusual correspondences between spelling and sound, and where these occur in the word.

Comprehension

C1	Pupils retrieve and record information from non-fiction.
C2	Pupils participate in discussion about both books that are read to them and those they can read for themselves, taking turns and listening to what others say.
Pupils develop positive attitudes to reading and an understanding of what they read by:	
C3	Listening to and discussing a wide range of fiction, poetry, plays, non-fiction and reference books or textbooks.
C4	Reading books that are structured in different ways and reading for a range of purposes.
C5	Using dictionaries to check the meaning of words that they have read.
C6	Increasing their familiarity with a wide range of books, including fairy stories, myths and legends, and retelling some of these orally.
C7	Identifying themes and conventions in a wide range of books.
C8	Preparing poems and play scripts to read aloud and to perform, showing understanding through intonation, tone, volume and action.
C9	Discussing words and phrases that capture the reader's interest and imagination.
C10	Recognising some different forms of poetry.
Pupils understand what they read, in books they can read independently, by:	
C11	Checking that the text makes sense to them, discussing their understanding and explaining the meaning of words in context.
C12	Asking questions to improve their understanding of a text.
C13	Drawing inferences such as inferring characters' feelings, thoughts and motives from their actions, and justifying inferences with evidence.
C14	Predicting what might happen from details stated and implied.
C15	Identifying main ideas drawn from more than one paragraph and summarising these.
C16	Identifying how language, structure and presentation contribute to meaning.

The following table should be used to record pupils' scores on the three summative assessment units.

Summative Assessment

Pupils' names	The Tale of Two Frogs			Life Cycle of a Mosquito			Catch that Cheese!																
	Comprehension (__/8)	Word Reading (__/12)	TOTAL (__/20)	Comprehension (__/10)	Word Reading (__/10)	TOTAL (__/20)	Comprehension (__/10)	Word Reading (__/10)	TOTAL (__/20)														
	Date:	Date:	Date:	Date:	Date:	Date:	Date:	Date:	Date:														

The following table should be used to record pupils' formative and summative assessments each term.

Year: **Term:**

Pupils' names	Red — Working towards expectations	Orange — Meeting expectations	Green — Exceeding expectations	Brief Description of Assessments Used — Formative	Brief Description of Assessments Used — Summative
	Date:	Date:	Date:		

Curriculum Links

Activity	Code	Objective	Outcome
Text	C3 C6 C13	• Listen to and discuss a wide range of fiction • Increase their familiarity with fairy stories, and retell some of these orally • Draw inferences such as inferring characters' feelings, thoughts and motives from their actions, and justifying inferences with evidence	• Can retell a story • Can offer an opinion about a character's behaviour
Comprehension	C5 C7 C11	• Use dictionaries to check the meaning of words they have read • Identify themes and conventions • Check that the text makes sense to them, discussing their understanding and explaining the meaning of words in context	• Can use a dictionary • Can recognise the theme of a piece of fiction • Can sequence events
Word Reading	WR1	• Apply their growing knowledge of root words	• Can identify a word's root • Can give another word similar in meaning • Can give the opposite of words

Additional Teacher Information

Definition of Terms

Narrative

A narrative is a text that tells a story. It includes a title, an orientation (setting, time and characters), a complication to the main character(s), a series of events, a resolution to the complication and an ending.

Fairy tale

A fairy tale is a form of narrative, often set in the distant past. Fairy tales usually begin with a phrase similar to 'Once upon a time ...' and end with similar words to '... and they lived happily ever after'. Besides people appearing in fairy tales, elves, dragons, other magical creatures and talking animals may be featured.

Links to other Curriculum Areas

• PSHE – Personal, social, health and economic education

Terminology for Pupils

fairy tale
adjective
antonym
root word
synonym

Suggested Reading

• These two books are based on the original story:
  Lazy Jack by Tony Ross
• This link is an oral retelling:
  <http://www.youtube.com/watch?v=d8p8u-9QV_g>
• This link is a visual retelling:
  <http://storyforkids24.blogspot.com.au/2013/04/folk-tale-lazy-jack.html>

Text

Teacher Information

- The fairy tale on page 5 is based on the 19th century English fairy tale by Joseph Jacobs, a folklorist, literary critic and historian. After leading an idle life for some time, Jack's mother finally insists he goes to work to help support them. He does this, but each time loses his payment through a series of comical mishaps by taking his mother's advice too literally. This pays off eventually, when he wins the hand of a young woman by unwittingly making her laugh.

Introduction

- Discuss fairy tales the class have heard/read before. Centre the discussion on common features (set in the past, beginning with the phrase 'Once upon a time' and ending with 'lived happily ever after', involving magical/mythical/far-fetched events). Scribe this list on the board as pupils discuss.

Development

- Read and discuss the text with pupils, as a whole class or in groups. Assist pupils to decode new words if necessary. Discuss the meaning of any new or unfamiliar words and phrases; e.g. yarn, spinning yarn, hearth, tomcat. Question individual pupils to gauge their understanding of what they have listened to or read.

- Pupils should also ask questions about parts of the text they are unsure of, in order to improve their understanding of it. Discuss the themes in the story such as the importance of working for a living, lack of common sense, and how luck can come your way in an unexpected manner.

Differentiated Individual/Paired/Group Work

- Ask pupils to come up with some other silly things that Jack could have done. They should write these in the same style of the story (e.g. On Monday, Jack worked for a .... He/She paid Jack with .... On the way home ....).

- Have some pupils create a diary entry from Jack's point of view. Have other pupils create a diary entry for the same day(s) from his mother's viewpoint.

Review

- Invite some pupils to read out their work and then invite comments from the other pupils.

- Have pupils think about the events in the story. Using a round robin approach, have one pupil begin the retelling, and have each subsequent pupil add the next event.

Comprehension

Teacher Information

- Pupils will need a dictionary to complete question 4.

Introduction

- Reread the fairy tale. Have pupils focus on the sequence of events. Ask them to try and remember the order of things that Jack received as payment.

Development

- Ask quick questions, such as: Why did Jack have to get a job? What did he do on Monday? What did his mother always exclaim? What kind of person was Jack?/his mother? Use evidence from the text.

- Discuss answers to questions that may have varied answers, especially questions 6 and 7. Pupils should be able to justify their answers to support a 'Yes' or 'No' decision.

- Discuss the comprehension activities on page 6, before pupils complete the page independently.

Differentiated Individual/Paired/Group Work

Less Able Readers	Highly Able Readers
• Make a comic strip of the story. In each box of the comic strip, show the silly things that Jack did. • Ask less able readers to pick their favourite part of the story, illustrate it and write a caption for their picture. • Assist a group of less able readers to orally summarise the main events of the story. Ask them to explain vocabulary from the story in their own words (e.g. exclaimed; permission; shabby).	• Write a short paragraph, from the point of view of the rich man's daughter, of the scene she saw on Monday. • Capable readers can work independently and read the story silently. They could then form pairs, taking turns to read Jack's mother's spoken part and the 'narrator's' part. • Ask pupils to predict what Jack and his new wife's life was like. They can write a paragraph outlining if Jack got a job, if he stopped doing silly things etc.

Review

- Bring the class together for a discussion about the characters (good points/weaknesses). The pupils should justify any opinions with evidence from the text and their wider knowledge.

Word Reading

Teacher Information

- The activities on page 7 focus on synonyms, antonyms and root words.

Introduction

- Reread the text, but this time explain to the pupils that the focus will be on words. As a different focus question while reading, ask pupils to underline any occupations that are mentioned in the text.

Development

- Discuss words that have similar meanings. Use words pupils have encountered before (for example, pretty/beautiful; smile/ grin). Teach pupils that words like these are called synonyms.

- Discuss words opposite in meaning. Try to use words already discussed as synonyms (for example, beautiful/ugly; smile/ frown). Teach pupils that words like these are called antonyms. Each time a new word is encountered, encourage the pupils to think of its synonym and its antonym. Display these on a classroom poster.

- Questions 7, 8 and 9 require pupils to focus on the roots of words. Root words are words that can stand alone. Root words can have suffixes and prefixes added to them. For example, in the word 'played', 'play' is the root word. Discuss other words and their roots with the pupils (helpful, unfair, magical, and so on).

- Discuss the word reading activities on page 7, before pupils complete the page independently.

Differentiated Individual/Paired/Group Work

Less Able Readers	More Able Readers
• Assist a group of less able readers to correctly use a dictionary. Show and explain how a dictionary can show pupils root words. • Have less able readers reread the story silently and underline all the different people mentioned in the story (e.g. Jack, mother, farmer, cheesemaker). The pupils can write these words in a list.	• The word *nice* is overused. Ask the pupils to come up with as many synonyms as possible for *nice*. The pupils could then create a classroom poster for display and reference. • Using the root words in question 8, challenge pupils to write other words that can be made from each root word.

Review

- Have the pupils write a list of common words. Ask the person sitting next to them for the synonyms of these words. Can they also find the antonyms of these words?

Assessment

C11	Ask the pupils to write a short summary of this fairy tale. Remind them to try and include the most important events in the correct order. Also remind them that a good summary does not have to include all the tasks that Jack did. They need to be sure that the summary mentions Jack, his mother and what happens at the end.
WR1	Present the following words to the pupils and ask them to write down each root word: faster, lives, talking, jumped, reading, slowest, permission
WR2	Draw a grid with the headings *Antonyms* and *Synonyms*. Write this list of words and ask pupils to put them in pairs and in the correct column: wobbled, ugly, pulled, cried, shabby, melt, pretty, careful, smallest, largest, scruffy, staggered, exclaimed, freeze, dragged, careless

Answers

Comprehension

1. (a) enjoy
2. (c) amusing
3. Answers should indicate that Jack lazed around instead of working.
4. (a) hearth: the floor around a fireplace
   (b) tomcat: a male cat
5. (d), (a), (c), (b)
6.–7. Answers will vary.

Word Reading

1. (c) did not mean to drop it
2. (c) wobbled
3. (b) scruffy
4. No
5. (a) cool   (b) largest
   (c) melt   (d) carefully
   (e) lead   (f) beautiful
6. (a) silly – clever
   (b) release – capture
   (c) poor – rich
7. (a) start   (b) large
   (c) drag   (d) spoke
8. (a) laughing (b) starts
9. permit

Lazy Jack – 1

Read the fairy tale.

Once upon a time, there was a boy named Jack who lived with his mother in a small cottage. They were very poor and Jack's mother earned some money by spinning wool to make yarn. Jack did not earn any money. All he did was lay in the sun during warm weather and sit by the hearth in cool weather.

One Monday morning, however, Jack's mother said, 'No porridge until you find some work!' So Jack got a job with a farmer. On Tuesday, he did odd jobs for a penny. On the way home, he accidentally dropped it in a stream.

'Silly boy!' exclaimed his mother. 'Put it in your pocket next time!'

On Wednesday, Jack worked for a farmer who kept cows. He paid Jack with a jar of milk. Jack put the jar into the largest pocket of his shabby jacket. The milk spilled out on his way home.

'Silly boy!' exclaimed his mother. 'Carry it on your head next time!'

On Thursday, Jack worked for a cheesemaker. He paid Jack with a large block of cream cheese. On the way home, the cream cheese began to melt and some stuck to his hair.

'Silly boy!' exclaimed his mother. 'Carry it in your hands next time!'

On Friday, Jack worked for a baker who paid him with a large tomcat. Jack started carrying it home carefully in his hands. But the cat began to wriggle and scratch him and he had to release it.

'Silly boy!' exclaimed his mother. 'Tie string around it and lead it next time!'

On Saturday, Jack worked for a butcher who paid him with a delicious leg of lamb. Jack tied string to it and dragged it behind him in the dirt.

'Silly boy!' exclaimed his mother. 'Carry it over your shoulder next time!'

On Monday, Jack worked for a cattle farmer. Jack was paid with a donkey, which he put over his shoulders. He staggered past the home of a rich man who had a beautiful daughter. The daughter had never spoken or laughed. But when she saw Jack she laughed and laughed! Her father was very happy and gave Jack permission to marry his daughter.

So Jack married the beautiful daughter. With his mother, they all lived happily ever after in a large mansion.

	After reading this fairy tale, I can remember:
My learning log	☐ all the events in the correct order.
	☐ most of the events in the correct order.
	☐ some of the events in the correct order.

Lazy Jack – 2

1. *Lazy Jack* was written for the reader to:

    (a) enjoy ☐   (b) learn something ☐   (c) follow instructions ☐

2. Circle the adjective that best describes this story.

    (a) scary   (b) sad   (c) amusing

3. Why do you think the story is called *Lazy Jack*?

    _____

4. Use a dictionary to write the meaning of these words.

    (a) hearth   _____

    (b) tomcat   _____

5. Order these events in the story from 1 to 4.

    (a) Jack dragged a leg of lamb behind him. ☐

    (b) Jack moved into a mansion. ☐

    (c) A farmer paid Jack with a donkey. ☐

    (d) Jack's mother told him to get a job. ☐

6. (a) Why did the rich man's daughter laugh at Jack?

    _____

    (b) Do you think anything else Jack did would have made her laugh?

    ☐ Yes ☐ No If yes, suggest what might have made her laugh.

    _____

    _____

7. Do you think Jack was a sensible person? ☐ Yes ☐ No
   Explain your answer.

    _____

    _____

My learning log	While doing these activities:		
	I found Q _____ easy.	I found Q _____ challenging.	I found Q _____ interesting.

Lazy Jack – 3

1. Jack dropped his penny 'accidentally'. This means Jack:

   (a) meant to drop it.

   (b) had an accident and dropped it.

   (c) did not mean to drop it.

2. Jack 'staggered' past the rich man's home with the donkey on his back. Which word could be used instead of 'staggered'?

   (a) skipped   (b) raced   (c) wobbled

3. Jack had a 'shabby' jacket. Which word could be used instead of 'shabby'?

   (a) smart   (b) scruffy   (c) sensible

4. Is the word 'permission' used correctly in this sentence? Yes | No

   The secret agent's permission was to find the missing laptop.

5. Find and write a word from the story that is an antonym for these.

   (a) warm _____   (b) smallest _____

   (c) freeze _____   (d) carelessly _____

   (e) follow _____   (f) ugly _____

6. These words are used in the story. Write an antonym for each one.

   (a) silly _____   (b) release _____   (c) poor _____

7. Find the root word used to make each word and write it on the line.

   (a) started _____   (b) largest _____

   (c) dragged _____   (d) spoken _____

8. Change each root word to complete the sentence.

   (a) We were all (laugh) _____ at the story.

   (b) Every day, Dad (start) _____ his car at seven o'clock.

9. What is the root word of 'permission'? _____

My learning log	*Colour:*	I can / can't find the root of most words.
		I know / don't know what a synonym is.
		I could explain / would find it difficult to explain what an antonym is.

How are Donkeys Different?

Curriculum Links

Activity	Code	Objective	Outcome
Text	C3 C9 C16	• Listen to and discuss a wide range of non-fiction • Discuss words and phrases that capture the reader's interest and imagination • Identify how structure and presentation contribute to meaning	• Can read an information text
Comprehension	C1 C12 C15	• Retrieve and record information from non-fiction • Ask questions to improve their understanding of a text • Identify main ideas drawn from one or more paragraph and summarise these	• Can summarise the main ideas from a non-fiction text
Word Reading	WR1 WR2	• Apply their growing knowledge of suffixes • Read further exception words, noting the unusual correspondences between spelling and sound	• Can use the suffix '-ous' • Can recognise and use different homophones

Additional Teacher Information

Definition of Terms

Explanation

An explanation is a text written in the form of a detailed description, which outlines how something occurs, works or is made. Its purpose is to inform the reader.

Paragraph

A distinct section of a piece of writing, usually dealing with a single theme and indicated by a new line, indentation or numbering.

Links to other Curriculum Areas

• Science – Different parts of animals' bodies have special functions for support, protection and movement

Terminology for Pupils

explanation
non-fiction
paragraph
word
sentence
definition
homophone
suffix

Suggested Reading

• The following link provides information about the differences between donkeys and horses. It is more suitable for the teacher, who can relate some of the facts to pupils:

<http://www.ehow.com/about_6527107_difference-between-horsesdonkeys.html>

• This link includes interesting donkey facts:

<http://www.mikesdonkeys.co.uk/facts.html>

Text

Teacher Information

- The explanation on page 11 explains some of the main differences between donkeys and horses.

Introduction

- Provide colour photographs of donkeys and horses for pupils to view and identify the similarities and differences as they read the text. Discuss any real-life experiences the pupils may have had with donkeys or horses.

Development

- Read and discuss the text with pupils, as a whole class or in groups. Assist pupils to decode new words if necessary. Discuss the meaning of any new or unfamiliar words and phrases; e.g. the scientific name for the horse family, 'Equidae', of which ponies and zebras are also part of; the colour 'bay'; 'predators' and 'steeplechase'. Question individual pupils to gauge their understanding of what they have listened to or read. Pupils should also ask questions about parts of the text they are unsure of, in order to improve their understanding of it.

- Identify the similarities and differences between these animals in the same family and the reasons for different adaptations. For example, donkeys' natural habitat is marginal desert areas so they did not live in close herds and they had to spread out to look for food which was sparse. They developed a loud bray that travelled long distances to keep in touch with their herd. Horses kept in close herds and didn't need a 'voice' louder than a whinny.

Differentiated Individual/Paired/Group Work

- Ask pupils to write a summary of the text under two different headings: one on donkeys and one on horses.
- Less able readers could write six lines of text.
- Highly able readers could write up to twelve lines.

Review

- Have the pupils summarise by asking them to contribute their points of the key features for the donkey. Scribe this on the board for the pupils to reread and add any missing information.

Comprehension

Teacher Information

- For the differentiated work, factual material (reference/non-fiction books, encyclopedias, etc.) on different animals would be very useful so pupils can undertake their own research on an animal of their choice.

Introduction

- Reread the explanation and pose quick true or false statements to the pupils. For example, *Donkeys are only coloured in shades of grey. Horses' ears are shorter than donkeys'. Donkeys are easily frightened. Donkeys dislike foxes.*

Development

- Discuss answers to questions that may have varied answers, such as question 6. Pupils will most likely decide donkeys are sensible, but can disagree if they justify their answers to support a 'stubborn' decision.
- Discuss the comprehension activities on page 12, before pupils complete the page independently.

Differentiated Individual/Paired/Group Work

Less Able Readers	Highly Able Readers
• Have pupils make a list of the features of a donkey. • Work with a group of less able pupils and divide them into pairs. Have each pupil reread the passage and ask each other questions based on the content.	• Have pupils create a simple grid with two columns like the one shown. Ask pupils to reread the passage so they can fill in as many features of the donkey and the horse as they can find. <table><tr><td>Donkey</td><td>Horse</td></tr><tr><td></td><td></td></tr><tr><td></td><td></td></tr><tr><td></td><td></td></tr></table> • Pupils can be asked to research and write a simple explanation piece on an animal of their choice.

Review

- Have the class come together as a whole and select a few pupils to share their lists with the rest of the class. Then invite comments from the other pupils.

Word Reading

Teacher Information

- The activities on page 13 focus on dictionary work, homophones and the suffix '-ous'.
- Pupils will need a dictionary to complete question 2.

Introduction

- Reread the passage and have the pupils underline the following words: 'steeplechase', 'predators' and 'various'.

Development

- Encourage pupils to focus on writing the dictionary definition in their own words. Pupils should also be encouraged to write precise sentences that demonstrate the correct meaning of the words.
- Revise the term 'homophone', which the pupils met in Year 2. Discuss some common pairs of homophones (for example, blue/blew; sea/see; sun/son). Reinforce the importance of the difference in meaning between each pair of words.
- Review the term 'suffix' by revising some common suffixes from Year 2 (-ment, -ness, -ful, -less, -ly). Introduce the suffix '-ous'. Explain that it conveys the sense of 'full of/possessing'. Use example words such as poisonous, joyous and dangerous.
- Question 6(d) explores the word 'adventure' which loses the 'e' when adding the suffix. Teach this rule with words such as fame, continue and adventure.
- Discuss the word reading activities on page 13, before pupils complete the page independently.

Differentiated Individual/Paired/Group Work

Less Able Readers	Highly Able Readers
• Give pupils extra practice material on homophones and near-homophones they have met in Year 2. Pay particular attention to the following: there/their/they're to/too/two be/bee one/won • Make flashcards of these words and ask pupils to point to the correct homophone when they hear a sentence containing the word. (e.g. Say 'The boy bought two comics'. Pupil points to 'two'.).	• Challenge the pupils to think of four other pairs of homophones not explored on the 'Word Reading' page. Can they put these words into sentences which show the different meaning of each homophone? • Ask pupils to create a poster showing the rules for adding the suffix '-ous'. Ensure the poster contains example words before and after the suffix has been added. Also ensure that pupils include the rule for words ending in 'e'.

Review

- Give the pupils a list of homophones; for example, *plane/plain*, *meet/meat*, *grate/great*. As a class, discuss the meaning of each word and verbally put each homophone into a sentence for the teacher to scribe onto the board.

Assessment

C9	Have pupils reread the text on page 11 and ask them to choose five words that they could use in their own writing. Ask them to write each word, write its meaning and then place it in a sentence to best show its meaning.
WR1	Give the pupils a list of words and ask them to rewrite them adding the suffix '-ous'. Include the words: mountain, joy, poison, prosper, danger, fame If they can include each word correctly in a sentence, note this in the assessment.

Answers

Comprehension

1. (c) learn something
2. Answers will vary; for example,
   To learn about the differences in colour between donkeys and horses.
3. (b) have longer ears
4. Teacher check
5. donkey: will stay still
   horse: will gallop away
6. Pupils are likely to say they are sensible because they won't do something if they think it's dangerous.
7. It is not likely a donkey would go show jumping as it does not like to jump over heights.
8. They protect the flocks or herds from predators like foxes.

Word Reading

1. (a) tougher   (b) louder   (c) coarser
2. Answers will vary; for example,
   (a) a horse race run on a racecourse having ditches and hedges as jumps.
   (b) animals that prey on and eat other animals
   (c) many different kinds
3. (a) frightened   (b) regularly
4. (a) hear   (b) mane   (c) tail
   (d) herd
5. (a) main   (b) tail   (c) here
6. (a) dangerous   (b) poisonous   (c) mountainous
   (d) adventurous

Read the explanation.

Donkeys and horses look very much alike. That's because they are related. Both animals are members of the horse family, Equidae. ('Equidae' comes from the Latin word, 'equus', meaning 'horse'). How can you tell the difference between donkeys and horses?

Most donkeys are coloured various shades of grey but they can be black, brown, white or spotted. The most common horse colour is bay, a shade of brown, with black on the mane, tail and lower legs.

Donkeys' ears are longer than horses' ears. Their large ears help to keep them cool. They also help them to hear over long distances. Donkeys make very loud braying sounds, 'hee-haw', while horses make a softer 'whinny' sound. A donkey's bray can be heard by other donkeys three kilometres away.

Donkeys have tougher hooves than horses and do not need shoes like horses. However, donkeys' hooves still need to be trimmed regularly. Donkeys' coats are longer and coarser than horses' coats.

Like horses, donkeys like to live in herds. Both animals eat plant matter, though donkeys eat tougher plants than horses.

Donkeys are not easily startled like horses. A horse will usually gallop away if it gets a fright. A donkey will freeze on the spot if frightened. It thinks about what to do next.

Donkeys are sometimes placed in a flock or herd of sheep, goats or cattle. It will protect the animals from predators such as foxes which donkeys strongly dislike. If a donkey senses a fox is nearby, it will bray to warn the herd and even attack the fox by kicking it with its forelegs.

It is said that donkeys are stubborn and won't do what you want them to. This is because a donkey won't move if it thinks it is dangerous to do so. For example, donkeys don't feel safe jumping over fences so they can't be trained to steeplechase like many horses can!

| **My learning log** | When I read this explanation, I could read: | ⬜ all of it. | ⬜ most of it. | ⬜ parts of it. |

How are Donkeys Different? – 2

1. This information text was mainly written for the reader to:

   (a) follow instructions ☐   (b) enjoy ☐   (c) learn something ☐

2. What is the main idea of the second paragraph?

   _____

   _____

3. Donkeys are different from horses because they:

   (a) make softer sounds. ☐   (b) have longer ears. ☐

   (c) like to live in herds. ☐   (d) do not need shoes. ☐

4. Summarise and list two differences between donkeys and horses.

   Difference 1: _____

   Difference 2: _____

5. Imagine a horse and a donkey are in the same field next to a barn. The barn door suddenly slams shut. What is each animal most likely to do?

   donkey: _____

   horse: _____

6. (a) Do you think donkeys are stubborn or sensible? _____

   (b) Explain your answer. _____

   _____

7. (a) Is it likely you would see a donkey showjumping? ⬭ Yes   ⬭ No

   (b) Why/Why not? _____

   _____

8. How can donkeys help with sheep, goats or cattle?

   _____

   _____

My learning log	While doing these activities:		
	I found Q _____ easy.	I found Q _____ challenging.	I found Q _____ interesting.

How are Donkeys Different? – 3

1. Circle the correct word in the following sentences.

   (a) Donkeys eat (smaller/sweeter/tougher) plants than horses.

   (b) Donkeys' voices are (higher/louder/softer) than horses' voices.

   (c) Donkeys' coats are (softer/darker/coarser) than horses' coats.

2. Using a dictionary, write a definition for the word on the first line. On the second line, write your own sentence using the word.

   (a) steeplechase _____

   _____

   (b) predators _____

   _____

   (c) various _____

   _____

3. Find words in the explanation piece which mean the same as the following.

   (a) scared _____   (b) often _____

4. Homophones are words that sound the same but are spelt differently. Write the words from the explanation that are homophones of these.

   (a) here _____   (b) main _____

   (c) tale _____   (d) heard _____

5. Use the correct homophones from question 4 for these sentences.

   (a) Always be careful on the _____ road.

   (b) The dog hurt his _____.

   (c) 'Please come over _____', said the teacher.

6. Rewrite these words adding the suffix '-ous'.

   (a) danger _____   (b) poison _____

   (c) mountain _____   (d) adventure _____

My learning log	Colour:	I [can] / [can't] use a dictionary to find words.
		I [understand] / [need more practice on] homophones.
		I [know] / [don't know] when to use the suffix '-ous'.

The Wise Old Donkey

Curriculum Links

Activity	Code	Objective	Outcome
Text	C3 C7 C9	• Listen to and discuss a wide range of fiction • Identify themes and conventions • Discuss words and phrases that capture the reader's interest and imagination	• Can retell a folk tale
Comprehension	C5 C14 C16	• Use dictionaries to check the meaning of words they have read • Predict what might happen from details stated and implied • Identify how language, structure and presentation contribute to meaning	• Can use a dictionary • Can predict based on information within the text
Word Reading	WR1	• Apply their growing knowledge of root words and prefixes	• Can identify the root of words • Can use the prefix 'dis-'

Additional Teacher Information

Definition of Terms

Narrative

A narrative is a text that tells a story. It includes a title, an orientation (setting, time and characters), a complication to the main character(s), a series of events, a resolution to the complication and an ending.

Folk tale

A folk tale is a form of narrative, often set in the distant past. They are stories which have been passed from one generation to the next, often originally by word of mouth rather than being written down. Folk tales may include sayings, superstitions, social rituals, legends or lore about the weather, animals or plants.

Links to other Curriculum Areas

• PSHE – Personal, social, health and economic education

Terminology for Pupils

folk tale
phrase
word
synonym
root word
sentence
prefix

Suggested Reading

• An online version can be found at:

<http://www.firstpeople.us/FP-Html-Legends/ThePetDonkey-Sioux.html>

Text

Teacher Information

- The folk tale on page 17 is based on a Native American Sioux tale. Donkeys have been used as beasts of burden for thousands of years and this tale shows how highly respected donkeys were considered (and still are today) as willing, dependable workers.

Introduction

- This unit could be completed after the previous unit on pages 8 to 13 so pupils are familiar with the characteristics of donkeys. Read and discuss the text with pupils, as a whole class or in groups. Assist pupils to decode new words if necessary.

Development

- Discuss the meaning of any new or unfamiliar words and phrases. Question individual pupils to gauge their understanding of what they have listened to or read. Pupils should also ask questions about parts of the text they are unsure of, in order to improve their understanding of it.

- Ask pupils questions such as the following: *Why was there a big celebration in the village? Where were the twins going to go on the donkey? What things did the twins' father say the donkey could carry? Was it a good choice to let the donkey carry the twins? Why?/Why not?*

Differentiated Individual/Paired/Group Work

- Pupils can be asked to compose five of their own questions on the folk tale and exchange these with another pupil.

- Very little information is provided about the incident with the gang of thieves. Working in groups, ask pupils to think about and predict what happened. This can be turned into a writing activity.

Review

- Ask the groups to come together. Each group presents their version of what happened during the incident with the thieves. All groups must evaluate and discuss the groups' ideas, ensuring that the predictions are in line with the story.

Comprehension

Teacher Information

- Pupils will need a dictionary to complete question 3.

Introduction

- Reread the folk tale and ask pupils to write questions that they can ask other pupils in the class based on the content.

Development

- Discuss the comprehension activities on page 18 before pupils complete the page independently.

- Question 2 asks pupils to sequence events from the story. Have pupils give an oral retelling of the folk tale's main points so they can have a clear understanding of the sequence.

- Question 6(b) encourages pupils to predict based on details from the passage. Ensure pupils realise that predictions must align with the stated or implied details of the text, and have to be justifiable according to these details.

Differentiated Individual/Paired/Group Work

Less Able Readers	Highly Able Readers
• Pupils can be asked to reread the story and underline any words they are not sure of. The teacher can discuss these words with the pupils. Pupils can add these words to their personal dictionary for future use.	• A writing task: pupils can be asked to summarise the folk tale in 100 words or less.

Review

- Have volunteers read their summaries of the folk tale.

Word Reading

Teacher Information

- The activities on page 19 focus on synonyms, root words and the prefix 'dis-'.

Development

- Ensure pupils are familiar with the term 'synonym'. Give some examples (rich/wealthy; start/begin). Elicit some examples from the pupils. After the pupils have completed question 1, ask them to reread the sentences containing the original words and substitute in the synonymous words.

- Revise the term 'root word'. Explore ways of finding the root from words (for example, softly, softer; confused, confusion).

- Teach that the prefix 'dis-' can be added to a word to form its opposite. Provide examples such as allow, continue, connect and respect.

- Discuss the word reading activities on page 19 before pupils complete the page independently.

Differentiated Individual/Paired/Group Work

Less Able Readers	Highly Able Readers
• Place the synonyms in question 1 in alphabetical order. • Ask pupils to come up with a list of common words and their opposites. The teacher can say a sentence and the pupil can say the sentence using the opposite word. (e.g. Teacher: 'It was a hot, sunny day.' Pupil: 'It was a cold, cloudy day.')	• Using five different words, pupils can be challenged to write a sentence containing the word and its opposite (with the prefix 'dis-'). For example: John always obeys his mother, but Mary often disobeys her father.

Review

- Review the rules for adding the prefix 'dis-' to a word.

Assessment

C3	Have each individual pupil retell the folk tale while other pupils are working on a group task. Listen to see if the pupil can retell the events in sequence and capture the main events.
C14	One of the group work activities was to have pupils work together to predict what happened when the thieves attacked the camping party. Have the pupils write a paragraph telling what happened.
WR1	Present a list of words to the pupils. Ensure that half of them can have the prefix 'dis-' added to them, but also include, in the other half, words that cannot take the prefix 'dis-'; for example, active, agree, appear, appoint, behave, correct, honest, infect, lead, legal, obey, spell

Answers

Comprehension

1. In and near the Sioux people's camp in North America.

2. (b), (a), (d), (c)

3. (a) supplies of food and other necessities
   (b) feeling shamed and not respected

4. The donkey was carrying the twins so it was important he did not stumble or slip.

5. the twins

6. (a) Answers should indicate:
   He was the grandmother's favourite donkey and was trustworthy and dependable.
   The twins' father was cross and didn't want the twins to ride on an old donkey instead of a young pony.

   (b) Possible answers:
   The grandmother knew she could depend on the donkey to look after the twins.
   The twins' father realised the donkey was dependable and had taken the twins safely home.

Word Reading

1. (a) large   (b) celebration
   (c) travel   (d) battle
   (e) desperately   (f) relate

2. (a) exclaim/claim (b) desperate
   (c) pass   (d) celebrate

3. (a) deciding   (b) exclaimed

4. (a) dis (b) not

5. (a) disobey   (b) disloyal   (c) disagree
   (d) dishonest   (e) disappear   (f) disinfect

6. (a) disappear   (b) dishonest   (c) disinfect
   (d) disloyal

7. disprecious, distrustworthy

The Wise Old Donkey – 1

Read the folk tale.

For thousands of years, donkeys have been of great help to people all over the world. This folk tale about a donkey comes from the Sioux people of North America.

There once was a Sioux chief's daughter who was one of a large family. She lived in a camp with her father and mother, brothers and grandmother. She also had aunts, uncles and cousins who lived a few days' travel away.

When the daughter grew up, she married a young man from another camp. Some time later, they had twin sons. There was a huge celebration in her father's camp and elsewhere in their village. Everyone came to see the twins and congratulate her and her husband.

When the twins were a few months old, the grandmother said the twins should be shown off to their other relatives. She made two saddlebags for the twins to travel in and put them over her favourite, elderly donkey's back.

'This particular donkey is patient, sure-footed and trustworthy', she said. 'He will carry the twins in the saddlebags on his back.'

But the twins' father didn't agree. 'My sons should ride on a young pony, not an old donkey!' he exclaimed. 'The donkey can carry our food, water, cooking utensils, tepee poles and tents.'

The donkey, however, did not like having this load on his back. He began to rear up, bray and kick until everything fell off. The grandmother explained that the donkey felt dishonoured he was carrying the provisions and not the precious twins. She put the twins in the saddlebags on the donkey and he stood calm and still once more.

The camping party soon set off on their travels. The next day, as they were passing by some thick bushes, a band of thieves came upon them. A long battle took place and finally the thieves fled. The camping party prepared to leave once more but the donkey and the twins were nowhere to be seen.

After searching desperately for hours, the group decided to return to their village to relate the terrible news. With much sorrow, they first went to the grandmother's tepee. There stood the faithful donkey with two smiling, precious bundles in his saddlebags.

| My learning log | When I read this folk tale, I could read: | ☐ all of it. | ☐ most of it. | ☐ parts of it. |

The Wise Old Donkey – 2

1. Where is the setting for this story?

_____

2. List these events in order from 1 to 4.

    (a)   The grandmother made some saddlebags.

    (b)   Twin boys were born.

    (c)   The camping party searched for the donkey
         and the twins.

    (d)   The donkey brayed and shook off the provisions.

3. Use a dictionary to write the meaning of these words.

    (a)   provisions _____

    (b)   dishonoured _____

4. Why was it important that the donkey was sure-footed?

_____

_____

5. What does the phrase 'two smiling, precious bundles' refer to?

_____

6. (a) What did the grandmother and the twins' father think about the donkey before the trip?

Grandmother	Twins' father

    (b)   What do you think the grandmother and the twins' father would have thought about the donkey at the end of the story?

Grandmother	Twins' father

My learning log	While doing these activities:		
	I found Q _____ easy.	I found Q _____ challenging.	I found Q _____ interesting.

The Wise Old Donkey – 3

1. Find and write a word from the story that is a synonym for these.

    (a) huge   _____   (b) party   _____

    (c) journey   _____   (d) fight   _____

    (e) frantically _____   (f) retell _____

2. Write the root word from which these words were made.

    (a) exclaimed   _____   (b) desperately _____

    (c) passing   _____   (d) celebration _____

3. Read these sentences and correctly change the root word.

    (a) I am still (decide) _____ what to order.

    (b) 'You shouldn't do that!' (exclaim) _____ the teacher.

4. (a) Circle the prefix in this word.   **dishonoured**

    (b) What does this prefix mean? _____

5. Rewrite these words by adding the prefix 'dis-'.

    (a) obey _____   (b) loyal _____   (c) agree _____

    (d) honest _____   (e) appear _____   (f) infect _____

6. Use the 'dis-' words from question 5 to fill in the blanks.

    (a) The magician made the rabbit _____.

    (b) The _____ salesperson took the woman's money.

    (c) We need to _____ the baby's bottle.

    (d) The _____ soldier gave away top-secret information.

7. Tick which of the following 'dis-' words are not real words.

    (a) disclaim   _____   (b) disprecious _____

    (c) distrustworthy _____   (d) disagree   _____

My learning log	*Colour:*	I [understand] / [need more practice on] synonyms.
		I [can find] / [can't find] the roots of many words.
		I [know] / [don't know] when to use the prefix 'dis-'.

The Three Sillies

Curriculum Links

Activity	Code	Objective	Outcome
Text	C3 C6	• Listen to and discuss a wide range of fiction • Increase their familiarity with fairy stories	• Can identify fairy tales and talk about their key features
Comprehension	C11 C13 C14	• Check that the text makes sense to them, discuss their understanding and explain the meaning of words in context • Draw inferences such as inferring characters' feelings, thoughts and motives from their actions, and justifying inferences with evidence • Predict what might happen from details stated and implied	• Can explain the meaning of phrases • Can explain characters' motives for their silly actions • Can predict what might happen if the story were to continue
Word Reading	WR1 WR2	• Apply their growing knowledge of suffixes • Read further exception words, noting the unusual correspondences between spelling and sound, and where these occur in the word	• Can identify words with '-ion' suffix • Can recognise the 'ou' sound • Can distinguish the spelling of different homophones

Additional Teacher Information

Definition of Terms

Narrative
A narrative is a text that tells a story. It includes a title, an orientation (setting, time and characters), a complication to the main character(s), a series of events, a resolution to the complication and an ending.

Fairy tale
A fairy tale is a form of narrative, often set in the distant past. Fairy tales usually begin with a phrase similar to 'Once upon a time ...' and end with similar words to '... and they lived happily ever after'. Besides people appearing in fairy tales, elves, dragons, other magical creatures and talking animals may be featured.

Paragraph
A distinct section of a piece of writing, usually dealing with a single theme and indicated by a new line, indentation or numbering.

Terminology for Pupils

fairy tale
title
homophone
sentence
paragraph
suffix
vowel sound

Suggested Reading

• These two books are based on the original story:
The Three Sillies by **Steven Kellogg**
The Three Sillies by **Paul Galdone**
• This link is an oral retelling of the story:
<http://www.youtube.com/watch?v=rJOnAXs244Y>

Links to other Curriculum Areas

• PSHE – Personal, social, health and economic education

Text

Teacher Information

- The fairy tale on page 23 is based on a 19th century English fairy tale by Joseph Jacobs, a folklorist, literary critic and historian. It is about a young man who has encounters with people that lack common sense, unlike the young man himself who is sensible and practical. While there are underlying themes in the story, its main purpose is for enjoyment.

Introduction

- Ask pupils if they have ever read, or have had read to them, a fairy tale. Ask them the names of the fairy tales and list them on the board. What features do fairy tales have in common? Do pupils have a favourite fairy tale?

Development

- Read and discuss the text with pupils, as a whole class or in groups. Assist pupils to decode new words if necessary. Discuss the meaning of any new or unfamiliar words and phrases. Question individual pupils to gauge their understanding of what they have listened to or read. Pupils should also ask questions about parts of the text they are unsure of, in order to improve their understanding of it.

- Discuss the practice of growing grass on the roof for insulation and to feed animals such as cows (especially in previous centuries). Find and view pictures on the Internet. Have any of the pupils seen a house with a grass roof?

- Discuss the themes in the story of common sense and lack of common sense, importance of keeping promises and acceptance of others' differences.

Differentiated Individual/Paired/Group Work

- Imagine that the young man said he would return after he had found four sillier things. What could the fourth silly thing be?

- Less able pupils could write a few sentences and draw an illustration.

- More able pupils could write an extra paragraph that could be included in the story, to tell about this fourth thing.

Review

- Pupils should share their work in a small group.

Comprehension

Introduction

- Pupils take it in turns to retell the fairy tale in their own words, sequencing the events correctly. They should also try to explain why the people did such silly things.

Development

- Discuss answers to questions that may have varied answers, especially question 6. Pupils should justify whether or not they think the couple would live happily ever after.

- Discuss the comprehension activities on page 24, then allow pupils to complete the page independently.

Differentiated Individual/Paired/Group Work

- Pupils write a list of silly things the daughter might have done once she was married. More able pupils could continue the story, a year after the couple got married.

- Pupils should share their ideas and/or stories in a small group.

Review

- As a class, compare pupils' answers to questions 4 and 6 as their answers will vary and will be interesting to compare.

Word Reading

Teacher Information

- The activities on page 25 focus on homophones, the suffix '-ion' and the vowel sound 'ou'.

- Pupils will need a dictionary to complete question 3.

Introduction

- Reread the text, but first explain to pupils that the focus will be on words. While reading, ask pupils to find the word ending in '-tion' and circle it. The word is 'reflection'.

Development

- Ensure pupils are familiar with the term 'homophone'. Give some examples (see/sea; there/their; maid/made). Elicit some examples from the pupils. Pupils suggest sentences for pairs of homophones, to be written onto the board; for example, son/ sun = My parents have a <u>son</u> and a daughter./Planet Earth orbits around the <u>sun</u>.

- Discuss and list words which end with the suffix '-ion', specifically the spelling '-tion'. This spelling is used if the root word ends in 't' or 'te'; for example, invention, injection, action, hesitation, completion. Sort the words according to whether the root word ends in 't' or 'te'. There are some exceptions; for example, the words 'attend' and 'intend' both end in 'd', but add the '-tion' suffix to become 'attention' and 'intention'.

- The 'ou' words in questions 4 and 5 should be spoken out loud, so pupils can hear the specific phonemes focused upon.

- Discuss the word reading activities on page 25, then allow pupils to complete the page independently.

Differentiated Individual/Paired/Group Work

- In pairs, pupils should find and list words with an '-ion' suffix; for example, 'invention', 'tension' and 'confession'. Then they should sort them according to their '-ion' ending, '-tion', '-sion' or '-ssion'. Less able pupils could sort the two types of '-ion' suffixes, '-tion' and '-sion'. More able pupils could also search for words ending in the suffix '-cian', which has the same sound.

'-tion' suffix (Used if root word ends in 't' or 'te')	'-sion' suffix (Used if root word ends in 'd' or 'se')	'-ssion' suffix (Used if root word ends in 'ss' or 'mit')
invention injection action hesitation completion	expansion extension comprehension tension	expression discussion confession permission admission

Review

- As a class, compare pupils' lists of '-ion' words. Which of the suffixes has the greatest number of words?

C3	Ask the pupils to write a short summary of this fairy tale using bullet points. Remind them to include the most important events, in the correct order. They need to be sure that the summary mentions the young man, the daughter, her parents, the other three sillies and the ending.
C11	Present the following list of words to the pupils and ask them to write a definition for each: supper, handsome, ridiculous, evening, cellar, son
WR2	Call out (or write on the board) the following words and have pupils place them in two different grids, according to the shared sound: trousers, trouble, cloud, young, round, country, mouse, loud, found, would, house, touch, double

Answers

Comprehension

1. (a) Possible answers: The farmer, his wife and daughter were three silly people./The man went to find three silly things.
   (b) Teacher check
2. It had been there a long while as it was covered in cobwebs.
3. (a) It means she went up very quickly.
   (b) Answers should indicate that as the woman and cow were joined by the string through the chimney, the weight of the cow falling off the roof caused the woman to be shot up the chimney.
4. Possible answer: The woman could climb the ladder and pull or cut some grass for the cow to eat.
5. The man who was trying to jump into his trousers.
6. Answers will vary.

Word Reading

1. (a) there   (b) some   (c) son
   (d) passed   (e) be   (f) so
   (g) way   (h) made   (i) inn
2. (a) cellar (b) morning (c) which (d) see, sea
3. (a) reflection (b) Teacher check (c) mirror
   (d) action, invention, injection
4. (a) crowded (b) trousers (d) around
5.

'ou' like 'young'	'ou' like 'around'
would	loudly
touch	found
	house
	trousers

The Three Sillies – 1

Read the fairy tale.

There once was a farmer and his wife who had a pretty daughter. A handsome young man had fallen in love with the daughter. He came to the farmhouse every evening to visit her and have supper.

One evening, the daughter went to the cellar to fetch some things. As she was walking back, she looked up and noticed an axe stuck in one of the beams, covered in cobwebs. The daughter had an awful thought.

'Suppose I was to get married to my handsome man and we had a son', she wondered. 'What if the axe was to fall as he passed by and kill him? How terrible that would be!'

She began to cry. Her parents came to see why she was upset. When she told them they too began to cry. When the man found out what was wrong, he laughed and pulled the axe out of the roof. He told them they were all very silly. The man said he would leave and only return if he could find three sillier things. Then he would come back and marry the daughter.

After a few days, he came upon a house with grass growing on the roof. A woman was attempting to get her cow up a ladder to eat the grass. She finally managed to do so. Then she tied string around the cow, passed the string down the chimney and went inside and tied the end to her wrist. In that way, she would know if the cow fell off the roof. The cow did fall, which made the woman shoot up the chimney and get stuck halfway. The man pulled her out and told her it was a ridiculous thing to do.

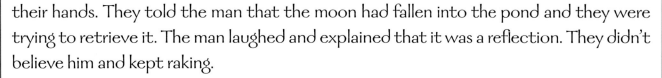

Next he came upon a group of villagers who were crowded around a pond with rakes and brooms in their hands. They told the man that the moon had fallen into the pond and they were trying to retrieve it. The man laughed and explained that it was a reflection. They didn't believe him and kept raking.

Later, the man stopped at an inn to spend the night. In the morning, he noticed a man had put his trousers over the knobs of a chest of drawers. He was running up and back across the room trying to jump into his trousers. The young man laughed loudly then showed the other man how to sit and put them on.

So the young man kept his promise and went back to the farm to marry the farmer's daughter. After all, she was no sillier than the others.

| **My learning log** | When I read this fairy tale, I could read: | ☐ all of it. ☐ most of it. ☐ parts of it. |

The Three Sillies – 2

1. (a) Why do you think the writer called the story *The Three Sillies*?

    _____

    _____

   (b) Write another suitable title.

    _____

2. The daughter saw an axe in the ceiling. Explain if you think it had been there a short while or a long while.

    _____

    _____

3. (a) The woman 'shot up the chimney'. What does this mean?

    _____

   (b) Why did the woman shoot up the chimney?

    _____

    _____

4. What would have been a sensible way to get the cow to eat the grass?

    _____

    _____

5. Which silly person accepted advice from the young man?

    _____

6. The man went back and married the daughter. Do you think they will live happily ever after? Explain your answer.

    _____

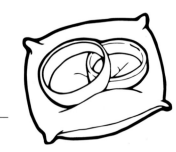

    _____

My learning log	While doing these activities:		
	I found Q _____ easy.	I found Q _____ challenging.	I found Q _____ interesting.

24 . . . . *Reading – Comprehension and Word Reading* . . . . • Prim-Ed Publishing • . . . . • www.prim-ed.com

The Three Sillies – 3

1. Which word from the text is a homophone for each word below?

   (a) their _____ (b) sum _____ (c) sun _____

   (d) past _____ (e) bee _____ (f) sew _____

   (g) weigh _____ (h) maid _____ (i) in _____

2. Underline the correct homophone in each sentence.

   (a) He went down into the wine (cellar / seller).

   (b) It was a beautiful, sunny (morning / mourning).

   (c) Do you know (witch / which) sandwich you want?

   (d) Look! I can (see / sea) the (see / sea)!

3. (a) Which word in paragraph 6 has the suffix '-ion'? _____

   (b) Use a dictionary to write the meaning of this word.

   _____

   (c) What do you use to see your reflection? _____

   (d) Add '-ion' to the following words.

   act _____ invent _____ inject _____

4. Say each word. Tick three words that have the same vowel sound.

   (a) crowded ☐ (b) trousers ☐ (c) young ☐ (d) around ☐

5. Write the following 'ou' words into the table according to their vowel sound.

   loudly   would   found   house   trousers   touch

'ou' like 'young'	'ou' like 'around'

My learning log	Colour:	I understand / need more practice on homophones.
		I know / don't know when to use the suffix '-ion'.
		I can read / am not too sure about the different 'ou' sounds in words.

Curriculum Links

Activity	Code	Objective	Outcome
Text	C3 C4	• Listen to and discuss a wide range of non-fiction and reference books • Read books that are structured in different ways	• Can identify key features of a non-fiction text
Comprehension	C5 C11 C16	• Use dictionaries to check the meaning of words that they have read • Check that the text makes sense to them, discuss their understanding and explain the meaning of words in context • Identify how language, structure and presentation contributes to meaning	• Can use a dictionary • Can write definitions for geographical words • Can read, understand and extract information in a table
Word Reading	WR1 WR2	• Apply their growing knowledge of root words, prefixes and suffixes • Read further exception words, noting the unusual correspondences between spelling and sound, and where these occur in the word	• Can find words with common prefixes • Can use the suffixes '-al' and '-ous' to change nouns to adjectives • Can recognise the /k/ sound spelt 'ch'

Additional Teacher Information

Definition of Terms

Report
Reports are written documents describing the findings of an individual or group about a specific subject.

Retrieval chart
A graphic organiser is used to record information. The items or criteria are written as a single word, phrase or statement in a heading. Important information is recorded relating to each criteria.

Heading
A heading tells the reader what a section of a text is about. It guides the reader through the text by showing the main idea of the sections being read. A heading is usually larger than the body text and is often in bold print.

Fact
Something that is true or real.

Opinion
A view or judgement formed about something, not necessarily based on fact or knowledge.

Links to other Curriculum Areas

• Geography – Name and locate geographical regions within the United Kingdom and identify human and physical characteristics

Terminology for Pupils

report
retrieval chart
non-fiction
definition
heading
fact
opinion
prefix
suffix
noun
adjective
antonym
synonym

Suggested Reading

• Reading and viewing globes, world maps, atlases and using Google Earth™ would assist pupils with this unit.

Text

Teacher Information

- The retrieval chart on page 29 provides facts about key physical and human features of the countries of Wales and Scotland. The chart is divided into headings, making it easier to read and comprehend the information and identify similarities and differences between the two countries.

Introduction

- Provide a globe, world map or map from an atlas for pupils to refer to. Explain how the United Kingdom is part of the continent of Europe and the countries that make up the UK are England, Scotland, Wales and Northern Ireland. Note: The term 'British Isles' is used if including the Republic of Ireland/Eire.
- Discuss experiences the pupils may have had with living, visiting or learning about each country.

Development

- Read and discuss the text with pupils, as a whole class or in groups. Assist pupils to decode new words if necessary. Discuss the meaning of any new or unfamiliar words and phrases. Question individual pupils to gauge their understanding of what they have listened to or read. Pupils should also ask questions about parts of the text they are unsure of, in order to improve their understanding of it.

Differentiated Individual/Paired/Group Work

- Pupils should be organised into mixed ability groups and given a topic to research about Scotland and Wales. Topics could include: traditional food, special celebrations, sporting events, historic buildings, national parks and facts about the capital cities.
- Each group should produce two factual posters on their topic, one for Scotland and one for Wales, with each pupil contributing to the poster.

Review

- Each group should present their posters to the rest of the class.

Comprehension

Introduction

- Pupils will need a dictionary to complete question 2 and the Internet or relevant reference books to complete question 3.
- Question 8 requires pupils to use their prior knowledge about mythical creatures, specifically the dragon and unicorn. Some discussion may be necessary.

Development

- Remind pupils how to use a dictionary efficiently; i.e. alphabetical order and retrieval by 1st, 2nd and 3rd letters. Give each pupil, or pair of pupils, a dictionary. Write words from the text onto the board for pupils to find.
- Discuss the comprehension activities on page 30, then allow pupils to complete the page independently.

Differentiated Individual/Paired/Group Work

- Pupils could create a glossary of geographical terms used in the text; for example, mountain, river, stream, lake, valley, hill, moorland, coast, cliff, beach.
- More able pupils could write a definition for each, list examples in the UK and provide an illustration. Less able pupils could create labelled illustrations.

Review

- Pupils share their glossaries with a group. They could discuss which place (mountain, valley, beach etc.) they would most like to visit, and why.

Word Reading

Teacher Information

- The activities on page 31 focus on the prefix 'kilo-', the suffixes '-al' and '-ous', synonyms and antonyms, and words with a 'k' sound.

Introduction

- Reread the text, but first explain to pupils that the focus will be on words. While reading, ask pupils to circle any words with a 'k' sound like 'kitten' or 'cake'. Discuss the spellings of these words.

Development

- Ensure pupils are familiar with the terms 'synonym' and 'antonym'. Give some examples (happy: synonym is glad, antonym is sad). Elicit some examples from the pupils. Pupils suggest sentences for pairs of synonyms and antonyms, to be written onto the board; for example, happy = glad/sad. Ben was glad he had homework, but Krista was sad.

- Look at words with the suffix '-ous'. Discuss that sometimes there is not an obvious root word; for example, 'poisonous' has the root word 'poison', but there is no root word for 'jealous'. Explain that whilst '-ous' can be added to many root words, '-our' is changed to '-or' before '-ous' is added; for example, humorous, glamorous.

- The 'k' words in question 6 should be spoken out loud, so pupils can hear the specific phoneme focused upon.

- Discuss the word reading activities on page 31, then allow pupils to complete the page independently.

Differentiated Individual/Paired/Group Work

- In pairs, pupils should find and list words with the following prefixes: 'kilo-', 'sub-', 'inter-', 'super-', 'anti-' and 'auto-'.

- Less able pupils should search for three of the prefixes, whilst the more able could search for all six.

- More able pupils could also research the meaning of each prefix; for example, 'kilo-' means a factor of 1000.

Review

- As a class, compare pupils' lists of words for each prefix. Which prefix had the most and least words?

Assessment

C4	Ask pupils to choose either Scotland or Wales, and write in prose, the information about that country. They should include at least one sentence about each section of the table.
C5	Present the following list of words to the pupils and ask them to write each in a sentence: mountain, kilometre, million, steep, beach, castle, thistle, kilt
WR1	Write the following words on the board and have pupils place them in two different grids, according to whether they need the suffix '-al' or '-ous' to change them from nouns to adjectives: magic, tradition, courage, accident, poison, nation, danger, mountain, coast

Answers

Comprehension

1. (a) Scotland   (b) Wales
2. (a) moorland   (b) tartan
3. Teacher check
4. (a) Physical features   (b) Location   (c) Population
5. Answers should indicate that the retrieval chart and headings make it easier to find the information and compare countries.
6. An opinion
7. Example of an answer: Similarity—both have mountainous regions. Difference—Scotland has exposed rocky shorelines and Wales does not.
8. No, because both animals are mythical creatures.

Word Reading

1. (a) Teacher check; Denoting a factor of 1000
   (b) Teacher check; kilogram, kilobyte, kilojoule
2. (a) al   (b) ous   (c) al   (d) al   (e) ous
   (f) al   (g) ous   (h) ous
3. (a) exposed   (b) sheltered
4. (a) east   (b) south   (c) north-west   (d) northern
   (e) largest   (f) wide   (g) male   (h) day
   (i) cold
5. (a) close   (b) largest   (c) many   (d) wide
   (e) regions (f) cold   (g) mixture   (h) solo
   (i) traditional
6. castle, cold, Cardiff, kilometres, chorus, echo, character

Wonderful Wales and Spectacular Scotland – 1

Read the information in the retrieval chart.

Wales' location

North-west Europe. Part of the United Kingdom.
Bordered by England to the east.

Scotland's location

North-west Europe. Part of the United Kingdom.
Bordered by England to the south.

	Wales	Scotland
Size	Close to 21 000 square kilometres	Close to 80 000 square kilometres. Includes nearly 800 islands.
Population	3.1 million	5.3 million
Capital city	Cardiff (largest city)	Edinburgh (largest city is Glasgow)
Physical features	Mostly mountainous. Cambrian Mountains spread over central and northern Wales. Many rivers, streams and lakes. Hills and moorland. Steep coastal cliffs. Wide sandy beaches.	Mountainous regions in the north. Many lakes, cold water rivers and streams. Central lowlands where most people live. Southern Uplands has hills and wide green valleys. Mixture of exposed rocky shorelines and sheltered ones.
National flag	Red dragon on a green and white field.	White cross on blue background.
National symbols	The leek and daffodil are national plants. Welsh harp is national instrument. Dragon is national animal.	Thistle is national flower. Bagpipes are national instrument. Unicorn is national animal.
Other interesting facts	Many castles across Wales. Called 'Land of Song' as known for harpists, male choirs and solo singers. National Day is St David's Day on 1 March.	Many castles across Scotland. Known for Highlanders wearing traditional tartan kilts and highland dancing. National Day is St Andrew's Day on 30 November.

My learning log	When I read this chart, I could read:	☐ all of it. ☐ most of it. ☐ parts of it.

Wonderful Wales and Spectacular Scotland – 2

1. Tick the correct country.

   (a) Larger country: Wales ☐   Scotland ☐

   (b) Smaller population: Wales ☐   Scotland ☐

2. Find a word in the text to match each definition.

   (a) open areas of damp, wild land   _____

   (b) checked or striped patterned material   _____

3. Find a photograph of each country's flag and use the correct shades to colour the flags on page 29.

4. Name the headings under which you would find the following information.

   (a) the landforms of each country   _____

   (b) where each country is found   _____

   (c) number of people who live in each country _____

5. Why has the writer presented the text in a table with headings?

   _____

6. Is the title of the text a fact or opinion? _____

7. List one similarity and one difference between the physical features of both countries.

Similarity	Difference

8. Would you be likely to see an actual dragon or unicorn in Wales or Scotland?

   ☐ Yes   ☐ No   Explain your answer.

   _____

   _____

My learning log	While doing these activities:		
	I found Q _____ easy.	I found Q _____ challenging.	I found Q _____ interesting.

Wonderful Wales and Spectacular Scotland – 3

1. (a) In the word 'kilometres', what does the prefix 'kilo-' mean?

    _____

    (b) Look in a dictionary. Write other words with the prefix 'kilo-'.

    _____

2. Add the suffix '-al' or '-ous' to these root words, to change the nouns to adjectives.

    (a) nation_____ (b) mountain_____ (c) coast_____ (d) tradition_____

    (e) danger_____ (f) magic_____ (g) poison_____ (h) courage_____

3. In the facts about Scotland in the *Physical features* section, find a word to match each definition.

    (a) unprotected from the weather _____

    (b) protected from the weather _____

4. Find a word from the text that is an antonym for these words.

    (a) west _____ (b) north _____ (c) south-east _____

    (d) southern _____ (e) smallest _____ (f) narrow _____

    (g) female _____ (h) night _____ (i) hot _____

5. Find a word from the text that is a synonym for these words.

    (a) near _____ (b) biggest _____ (c) lots _____

    (d) broad _____ (e) areas _____ (f) cool _____

    (g) variety _____ (h) individual _____ (i) historic _____

6. Circle the words that have a 'k' sound like 'kitten'.

castle	chorus	cold	Cardiff	machine	beaches
choir	kilometres	echo	chef	character	cheese

My learning log	*Colour:*	I [understand] / [need more practice on] synonyms and antonyms.
		I [know] / [don't know] when to use the suffixes '-al' and '-ous'.
		I [can read] / [am not too sure about] the different 'k' sounds in words.

Wonderful Welsh Cakes

Curriculum Links

Activity	Code	Objective	Outcome
Text	C3 C4	• Listen to and discuss a wide range of non-fiction and reference books • Read books that are structured in different ways and read for a range of purposes	• Can discuss the layout and vocabulary used in a procedure
Comprehension	C11 C16	• Check that the text makes sense to them, discuss their understanding and explain the meaning of words in context • Identify how language, structure and presentation contribute to meaning	• Can use a dictionary to find and check word meanings • Can identify sections of a recipe • Can sequence steps in a procedure
Word Reading	WR1	• Apply their growing knowledge of root words and suffixes	• Can use the suffix '-ly' to create new words

Additional Teacher Information

Definition of Terms

Report

Reports are written documents describing the findings of an individual or group about a specific subject.

Procedure

A procedure is a text that outlines how something is made or done. Its purpose is to inform the reader. A procedure may be written in the form of a recipe, instructions for making something, an experiment, how to play a game, how to use an appliance and so on. A procedure usually includes numbered, concise instructions beginning with imperative verbs.

Links to other Curriculum Areas

• History – Investigating food trends over time

• Design and Technology – Prepare and cook Welsh cakes

Terminology for Pupils

procedure
recipe
non-fiction
illustration
root word
suffix
adjective
adverb

Suggested Reading

• Using a search engine, pupils can locate variations of this recipe online.

Text

Teacher Information

- The procedure on page 35 is a recipe for the traditional Welsh food of Welsh cakes or Bakestones. A 'bake stone', a flat stone placed over an open fire, was traditionally used to cook the cakes. Now a modern equivalent such as an iron griddle plate is used as it too gives a continuous even distribution of heat.

Introduction

- Colour photographs of Welsh cakes (from the Internet) or homemade Welsh cakes could be shown (or tasted!) by pupils prior to reading the text. Some pupils may already be familiar with Welsh cakes. (Foods like crumpets and pancakes are similarly cooked.)

Development

- Read and discuss the recipe with the pupils. Assist pupils to decode new words if necessary. Question individual pupils to gauge their understanding of what they have listened to or read. Pupils should also ask questions about parts of the text they are unsure of, in order to improve their understanding of it.
- Discuss the meaning of any new or unfamiliar words and phrases. Some vocabulary is subject-specific relating to recipes.
- Discuss the layout of the procedure/recipe with pupils so they can see how numbered, concise steps make it easier to follow the instructions. The instructions usually begin with an imperative (command) verb.

Differentiated Individual/Paired/Group Work

- Pupils write a procedure for completing an everyday classroom task; for example, sharpening a pencil, getting a dictionary off the bookshelf, rubbing out an error on a piece of paper.
- Less able pupils could work in pairs to write their instructions.
- More able pupils need to have at least five steps to complete their task.

Review

- Pupils should test their procedure on another pupil. Was the pupil able to follow the instructions or were there problems?

Comprehension

Teacher Information

- Pupils might need a dictionary to complete question 3.

Introduction

- Discuss the structure of the recipe. Talk about why the *Ingredients* and *Equipment* sections are useful, and why these things need to be collected before making the cakes. Discuss why the numbered steps in the *Method* section make it easier to follow the recipe.

Development

- Remind pupils how to use a dictionary efficiently; i.e. alphabetical order and retrieval by 1st, 2nd and 3rd letters. Give each pupil, or pair of pupils, a dictionary. Write words from the text onto the board for pupils to find.
- Discuss the comprehension activities on page 36, then allow pupils to complete the page independently.

Differentiated Individual/Paired/Group Work

- Give pairs of pupils the ten points of the recipe, cut up into ten separate sections, without the number labels. Ask them to place the ten steps in the correct order.
- Less able pairs could just be given steps 1, 4, 5, 6, 9 and 10 to sequence.

Review

- As a class, discuss whether any of the steps were difficult to place in the correct order. Why was this?

Word Reading

Teacher Information

- The activities on page 37 focus on root words, the suffix '-ly', adjectives, adverbs and the suffix '-ish' for nationalities.

Introduction

- Explain to the pupils that they will reread the text, this time focusing on features of words. As they reread, ask them to find and underline the word with the suffix '-ly' (lightly).

Development

- Look at words with the suffix '-ly'. Tell pupils that this suffix is added to an adjective to form an adverb. Explain that usually the suffix is added straight onto the end of most root words; for example, sadly, finally. However, there are exceptions, which should also be explained to the pupils:

  (1) If the root word ends in '-y' with a consonant letter before it, the 'y' is changed to 'i', but only if the root word has more than one syllable; for example, happily.

  (2) If the root word ends with '-le', the '-le' is changed to '-ly'; for example, simply.

  (3) If the root word ends with '-ic', '-ally' is added rather than just '-ly'; for example, basically. An exception is 'publicly'.

  (4) The words truly, duly and wholly.

- Pupils complete the word reading activities on page 37 independently.

Differentiated Individual/Paired/Group Work

- In pairs, pupils should research the names given to people from different countries; i.e. their nationalities. The nationalities in question 5 all end in '-ish'. How many other endings are used for nationalities?

- More able pupils could try and discover whether certain parts of the world are more likely to have certain endings than others; for example, the '-ish' suffix is mainly used for European nations and '-i' for nations in the Middle East.

Review

- As a class, list the names of nationalities, in a table, according to suffix. Which suffix appears to be the most and least common for nationalities?

Assessment

C4	Ask the pupils to write a procedure for completing an everyday task they might do at home; for example, brushing their teeth, making toast, emptying the bin. Remind them that a procedure needs to have clear steps, in the correct order. They need to ensure that each step starts with an imperative (command) verb.
C11	Present the following list of words to the pupils and ask them to write a definition for each: sultana, cinnamon, sieve, spatula, dough
WR1	Write the following pairs of words on the board: kind/kindly, sad/sadly, greedy/greedily, angry/angrily Ask the pupils to write each pair of words in a sentence.

Answers

Comprehension

1. (a) Yes (b) The writer has used words like 'wonderful', 'delicious' and 'Eat and enjoy!' to describe them.
2. They are traditionally cooked on a bake stone over a fire.
3. grooved
4. It makes it easier and clearer to follow the instructions.
5. (6) Roll out the dough until it is about 1½ cm thick.
6. (c) Sugar and cinnamon are added.
7. The Welsh cakes could stick to the griddle.
8. To suggest other ways to serve the Welsh cakes.

Word Reading

1. (a) light   (b) flavour   (c) flute
   (d) originate/origin (e) beat   (f) grease
   (g) eat   (h) cook   (i) tradition
   (j) raise   (k) dust   (l) serve
   (m) mix   (n) roll   (o) measure
2. (a) lightly   (b) traditionally (c) firmly
   (d) thickly   (e) warmly   (f) wonderfully
3. heavily
4. Teacher check
5. (a) England   (b) Ireland   (c) Scotland
   (d) Spain   (e) Denmark   (f) Sweden

Wonderful Welsh Cakes – 1

Read the recipe.

Have you ever eaten a Welsh cake? These delicious little cakes originated in Wales. They are flavoured with dried fruit and spice and cooked on a flat, heavy griddle. Welsh cakes are also known as Bakestones in Wales as they are traditionally cooked on a bake stone over a fire.

Ingredients

- 2 cups self-raising flour
- ½ cup butter
- ½ cup sugar
- ⅔ cup sultanas
- 1 large egg (beaten)
- pinch cinnamon
- extra butter for greasing
- extra sugar for dusting

Equipment

- measuring cups
- sieve
- fork to beat egg
- large mixing bowl
- spatula
- rolling pin
- fluted cutter
- griddle plate

Method

1. Sieve flour into mixing bowl.

2. Add butter and rub it into flour with fingers.

3. Add sugar and cinnamon and use spatula to mix in.

4. Make a well in centre. Add beaten egg and sultanas.

5. Mix to make a firm dough.

6. Roll out the dough until it is about 1½ cm thick.

7. Cut into rounds. (Makes about 12.)

8. Lightly grease griddle and place it over direct heat.

9. Cook Welsh cakes for about 4 minutes on both sides until golden.

10. Dust with sugar while still warm. Eat and enjoy!

Note: Instead of dusting with sugar, cakes can be served with butter and jam.

My learning log	When I read this recipe, I could read:	☐ all of it. ☐ most of it. ☐ parts of it.

Wonderful Welsh Cakes – 2

1. (a) Do you think the writer likes Welsh cakes? Yes   No

   (b) Why do you think this? _____

   _____

   _____

2. Explain why Welsh cakes are sometimes called Bakestones.

   _____

   _____

3. A fluted cutter is one that has a _____ edge.

   | straight | grooved | pointy |

4. Why is the 'Method' section of a recipe written in steps?

   _____

   _____

5. Write the number and step this illustration shows.

   _____

   _____

6. Tick which happens first in the recipe.

   (a) A well is made in the mixture.   ☐

   (b) The dough is rolled out.   ☐

   (c) Sugar and cinnamon are added. ☐

7. What do you think would happen if the griddle wasn't greased?

   _____

8. What is the main idea of the 'Note' at the end of the recipe?

   _____

My learning log	While doing these activities:		
	I found Q _____ easy.	I found Q _____ challenging.	I found Q _____ interesting.

Wonderful Welsh Cakes — 3

1. Write the root word from which these words were made.

(a) lightly _____ (b) flavoured _____ (c) fluted _____

(d) originated _____ (e) beaten _____ (f) greasing _____

(g) eaten _____ (h) cooked _____ (i) traditionally _____

(j) raising _____ (k) dusting _____ (l) served _____

(m) mixing _____ (n) rolling _____ (o) measuring _____

2. Add the suffix '-ly' to these root words to change the adjectives to adverbs.

(a) light _____ (b) traditional _____ (c) firm _____

(d) thick _____ (e) warm _____ (f) wonderful _____

3. The word 'heavy' ends in '-vy'. The suffix '-ly' is added in a different way.

How is the adverb for 'heavy' written? _____

4. Write each adjective and adverb in a sentence.

(a) warm _____

warmly _____

(b) light _____

lightly _____

5. If you are Welsh, it means you come from Wales. Write the name of the country these people are from.

(a) English _____ (b) Irish _____

(c) Scottish _____ (d) Spanish _____

(e) Danish _____ (f) Swedish _____

My learning log	**Colour:**	I ⬡understand⬡ / ⬡need more practice on⬡ root words. I ⬡know⬡ / ⬡don't know⬡ when to use the suffix '-ly'. I ⬡can read⬡ / ⬡am not too sure about⬡ adjectives and adverbs in sentences.

Read this version of a folk tale from Japan.

Long ago in the country of Japan, there lived two frogs. One lived in a muddy puddle in a ditch near Osaka, which is on the coast. The other lived in a clear, flowing stream in Kyoto, which is inland.

The two frogs did not know each other but they shared the same dream. Both wanted to see a bit more of the world. The frog from Osaka wanted to visit Kyoto and the frog from Kyoto wanted to visit Osaka. By chance, they decided to set off to fulfil their dreams on the same spring morning.

In between the two places, a high mountain had to be crossed. Each frog took many hops and huffed and puffed a lot while trying to reach the mountain top. Finally, the two exhausted frogs made it to the summit. What a surprise they got to see another frog on the mountain peak!

'Hello!' croaked the frog from Osaka. 'I'm travelling to Kyoto.'

'Fancy that!' the frog from Kyoto croaked back. 'I'm on my way to Osaka.'

The two frogs decided to rest in the cool, damp grass before continuing their journey.

'What a shame we're not taller', croaked the frog from Osaka. 'If we could see over the grass we could look at both places from here. Then we could decide if the long journey ahead was worth it.'

'I have an idea', croaked the frog from Kyoto. 'If we stand on our hind legs, face each other and hold each other up, we could look at each place.'

So up they hopped and did just that, excited at what they would see. But they forgot one thing. While both faced towards the place they wanted to go to, the frogs could not see the place of their dreams. Frogs' eyes are set so far back in their heads that when they looked down, they were both actually looking at their own places.

'Goodness me!' croaked the frog from Osaka. 'Kyoto looks just like Osaka!'

'Indeed! Osaka is exactly like Kyoto', the frog from Kyoto croaked back.

The two frogs decided there was no point in visiting the other place. They said goodbye to each other and set off down each side of the steep mountain. Each frog was content to think that his home was as good as any other.

The Tale of Two Frogs

1. What did the two frogs have in common? Tick one.

   They lived in the same town. ☐   They lived in a stream. ☐

   They lived the same dream. ☐   They lived on the coast. ☐

   ☐ 1 mark

2. Find and copy the two words in paragraph 3 that describe the noises the frogs made while climbing the mountain.

   _____   _____

   ☐ 1 mark

3. Sequence these events from 1 to 4.

   (a) The frogs were surprised to see each other. ☐

   (b) Both frogs set off towards the mountain. ☐

   (c) The frogs stood on their hind legs. ☐

   (d) The frogs wished they were taller. ☐

   ☐ 2 marks

4. Tick the best answer. This text was written for the reader to:

   learn about frogs. ☐   enjoy a story. ☐   follow directions. ☐

   ☐ 1 mark

5. Describe the setting where most of this folk tale takes place.

   _____

   ☐ 1 mark

6. Write a word from the last paragraph that describes how the frogs felt as they hopped home.

   _____

   ☐ 1 mark

7. What would the frogs have seen if they stood back to back instead of facing each other on the mountain?

   _____

   _____

   ☐ 1 mark

Total for this page	/8

The Tale of Two Frogs

Assessment – Word Reading

1. Both frogs set off to 'fulfil their dreams'. What does this phrase mean?

_____

`2 marks`

2. Which word in paragraph 3 means 'mountain top'?

`1 mark`

3. Tick the word made from each root word found in the folk tale.

`1 mark`

(a) **travel**   travelled ☐   travelling ☐

(b) **excite**   excited ☐   exciting ☐

4. (a) Tick the correct box. The words 'damp' and 'dry' are

synonyms. ☐ antonyms. ☐

`1 mark`

(b) Tick the correct box. The words 'muddy' and 'dirty' are

synonyms. ☐ antonyms. ☐

`1 mark`

5. Circle the 'ou' word that has a vowel sound like 'ar<u>ou</u>nd'.

country   journey   mountain   could

`1 mark`

6. These words are in paragraph 1. Find each word's antonym which is also in paragraph 1.

`1 mark`

(a) coast _____   (b) muddy _____

7. The two frogs were '**exhausted**' when they reached the top of the mountain. Which word or phrase could best be used instead?

`1 mark`

(a) surprised ☐ (b) tired out ☐   (c) huffed and puffed ☐

8. Circle the suffix in this word. **finally**

`1 mark`

9. Tick the word that the suffix '-ous' can be added to.

`1 mark`

inland ☐   coast ☐   mountain ☐

10. Which word in the folk tale means 'a long trip'? _____

`1 mark`

Total for this page	/12	Total for this assessment	/20

The Tale of Two Frogs

Genre: Folk tale from Japan

Breakdown of question type/content and mark allocation

Comprehension			Word Reading		
Q 1.	Noting similarities	1 mark	Q 1.	Understanding phrases from context	2 marks
Q 2.	Understanding words	1 mark	Q 2.	Word meanings	1 mark
Q 3.	Sequencing	2 marks	Q 3.	Root words	1 mark
Q 4.	Point of view and purpose	1 mark	Q 4.	Understanding the terms *synonym* and *antonym*	2 marks
Q 5.	Finding information	1 mark	Q 5.	Words with 'ou' (as in 'around' vs 'young')	1 mark
Q 6.	Understanding words	1 mark	Q 6.	Word meanings (antonyms)	1 mark
Q 7.	Inferring	1 mark	Q 7.	Word meanings (synonyms)	1 mark
			Q 8.	Suffix '-ly'	1 mark
			Q 9.	Suffix '-ous'	1 mark
			Q 10.	Word meanings (synonyms)	1 mark
	Sub-total			Sub-total	
				Record the pupil's total result for this assessment.	

Assessment Answers

Assessment – The Tale of Two Frogs

Comprehension .... Page 39

1. They lived the same dream.
2. huffed, puffed
3. (b), (a), (d), (c)
4. enjoy a story
5. On the summit of a steep mountain
6. content
7. They would have seen each other's city instead of their own city.

Word Reading .... Page 40

1. make their dream come true/actually happen
2. summit
3. (a) travelling   (b) excited
4. (a) antonyms   (b) synonyms
5. mountain
6. (a) inland   (b) clear
7. (b) tired out
8. -ly
9. mountain
10. journey

Ferocious Dragons

Curriculum Links

Activity	Code	Objective	Outcome
Text	C3 C8 C10	• Listen to and discuss a wide range of poetry • Prepare poems to read aloud and to perform, showing understanding • Recognise some different forms of poetry	• Can read a poem with fluency and expression
Comprehension	C9 C11	• Discuss words and phrases that capture the reader's interest and imagination • Check that the text makes sense to them, discuss their understanding and explain the meaning of words in context	• Can write words from the poem that match definitions
Word Reading	WR1 WR2	• Apply their growing knowledge of suffixes • Read further exception words, noting the unusual correspondences between spelling and sound, and where these occur in the word	• Can divide words containing '-ture' into syllables and read them • Can distinguish homophones and near-homophones

Additional Teacher Information

Definition of Terms

Poetry
Poetry is a genre which utilises rhythmic patterns of language. The patterns include metre (high-low stressed syllables), syllabification (the number of syllables in each line), rhyme, alliteration, or a combination of these. Poems often use figurative language.

Cohesion
Grammatical or lexical relationships that make links between different parts of a text and hold it together. Cohesion is achieved through devices such as paragraphs, connectives, ellipses and word associations.

Figurative language
Words are used to create mental images and impressions by comparing ideas. These comparisons help the reader to imagine the person, place or thing being described.

Simile
A simile compares one thing with another. Similes make a description more emphatic or vivid. Similes are usually introduced by the words 'like' or 'as'.

Terminology for Pupils

poem
verse
line
rhyme
simile
syllable
synonym
homophone/near-homophone

Suggested Reading

• A collection of dragon poetry can be found at:
  <http://hellopoetry.com/words/9924/dragon/poems/>

Text

Teacher Information

- The poem on page 45 is a quatrain; i.e. a poem of four lines per verse or stanza. The poet has used an ABCB rhyming pattern where the second and fourth lines rhyme. Effective imagery has been obtained through the use of adjectives in descriptive phrases to describe a dragon's characteristics and figurative language with the use of similes. Each verse ends with an exclamation mark for emphasis and dramatic effect.

Introduction

- Discuss features of poems with the class. On the whiteboard, scribe the features the class collectively come up with. Discuss rhyming words.

Development

- Read and discuss the poem with pupils, as a whole class or in groups. Assist pupils to decode new words if necessary. Discuss the meaning of any new or unfamiliar words and phrases. Question individual pupils to gauge their understanding of what they have listened to or read. Pupils should also ask questions about parts of the poem they are unsure of, in order to improve their understanding of it.

- Give the pupils, in mixed-ability groups, sticky notes and pens. Ask each group to pick some words from the poem (brave, leg, snake) and ask them to think of as many different rhyming words as possible.

Differentiated Individual/Paired/Group Work

- Have mixed-ability groups take the poem and come up with different ways to read the poem (choral reading, reading alternate lines, having some pupils emphasise key words). Allow groups time to practise.

- Have highly able readers compose another poem about a creature (dinosaur, ogre, etc.). Less able readers could take the poem provided and highlight each pair of rhyming words.

Review

- Bring the whole class together and have each group read the poem in the way their group decided.

Comprehension

Teacher Information

- The cohesive device of using different words to refer to the same subject or word associations ('dragons'/'towering, terrifying animals'), is the focus of question 3.

Introduction

- Reread the poem, having pupils read it in unison. Ensure pupils are comfortable with the new vocabulary. Ask some pupils to give sentences with the words 'emit', 'gruesome', 'dreary', 'surrounding' and 'dwell' in them.

Development

- Discuss the rhyming pattern, use of imagery and exclamation marks in the poem.

- Ensure pupils understand the concept of main idea. Question 4 asks pupils to find the main idea in a particular verse. Compare their answers to question 6(c) as answers will vary. Question 7 asks pupils to review what they did in the previous lesson, but this time from an individual perspective. They will also need some guidance on voice expression and the role of gestures and actions to enhance a poem's delivery.

- The teacher may have to work individually with less confident readers to help them prepare their verse for reading.

- Discuss the comprehension activities on page 46, before pupils complete the page independently.

Differentiated Individual/Paired/Group Work

- Have pupils write as many vocabulary words in one sentence as possible; e.g. The ferocious, gigantic dragon emitted a powerful roar that frightened the terrified villagers.

- Have highly able readers make a list of some similes using the framework: as _____ as _____. For example, as fast as lightning.

Review

- Invite some individual pupils to perform their favourite verse from the poem.

Word Reading

Teacher Information

- The activities on page 47 are designed to support the development of vocabulary with a variety of word reading exercises. They include syllabification to assist in reading words and understanding homophones and near-homophones.

Introduction

- Revise the concept of syllabification and ensure pupils are familiar with dividing lines to mark out the syllables. All the parts of question 1 focus on words with two or three syllables. Tell pupils that some words can have only one syllable (mouth, eyes). Have pupils read the poem and ask them to find three words with one syllable, three words with two syllables and three words with three syllables.

Development

- Have pupils complete question 1 independently. They will notice that all the words selected for syllabification end in '–ture', which is also the focus for question 2.

- Introduce homophones and then discuss near-homophones. Common homophones the pupils will have covered previously include (son/sun; I/eye). Use other near-homophones to illustrate the concept.

- Pupils complete the word reading activities on page 47 independently.

Differentiated Individual/Paired/Group Work

Less Able Readers	Highly Able Readers
• Provide extra help and practice with syllabification to those pupils who need it. Use the poem as a basis for the words chosen. • Have pupils illustrate the content of stanzas three and four.	• Have pupils write the '-ture' words in sentences that display their meaning. • Have pupils make definition cards (both in writing and pictorially) for these homophones (night/knight, mare/mayor, hair/hare, flour/flower).

Review

- Ask the pupils to come up with rules for syllabification based on the work done today.

Assessment

C8	Give each pupil a new copy of the poem and ask them to silently prepare a verse for performance. Have each pupil 'perform' their verse. Note down accuracy of reading, intonation and use of gesture/facial expression.
WR1	Have pupils listen to the following syllable 'sums' to write the words correctly: pic + ture ad + ven + ture fur + ni + ture de + par + ture sig + na + ture
WR2	Provide the pupils with sentences containing gaps where there are missing words. Ask them to fill in the correct homophone: their/they're/there. I see my friend over _____. _____ all going to the party, so why can't I? Is that _____ new house?

Answers

Comprehension

1. (b) second and fourth
2. (a) ferocious   (b) gruesome   (c) emit
3. dragons
4. Answers should indicate that dragons emit fire so powerfully that it would kill anything within range.
5. (a) wings like bats   (b) scales like lizards
   (c) tails like serpents
6. (a) Yes
   (b) The writer talks about dragons as if they are real; e.g. he/she says if you want to visit one you must be extremely brave/keep your distance if one is living near you.
   (c) Teacher check
7. Teacher check

Word Reading

1. na/ture, fu/ture, mix/ture, pic/ture, fur/ni/ture, de/par/ture, ad/ven/ture, sig/na/ture
2. (a) furniture   (b) picture   (c) departure
3. (a) emit   (b) dwell   (c) dreary
   (d) gigantic/towering
4. Teacher check   (d) Their, there, they're
5. (a) breath   (b) breathe

Read the poem.

Dragons are ferocious creatures
Who dwell in dark and dreary caves
If you want to visit one
You must be extremely brave!

These towering, terrifying animals
Hatch from gigantic, stony eggs
That are as long as one metre
About the length of one man's leg!

Dragons have scales like lizards
Massive wings so they fly like bats
Tails that stretch like serpents
Gruesome claws much sharper than cats!

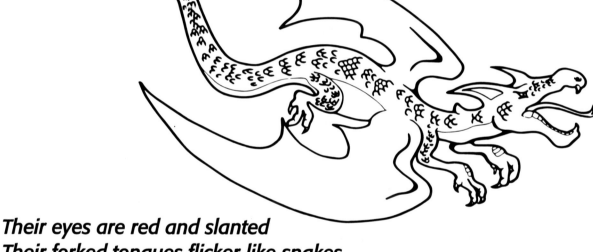

Their eyes are red and slanted
Their forked tongues flicker like snakes
The roar they emit from their mouth
Makes the surrounding earth shake!

Dragons breathe out fire
In such a powerful blast
That anything in its path
Would certainly not last!

If you should discover
That a dragon is living near you
Be sure to keep your distance
I'm sure you'd agree too!

My learning log	When I read this poem, I could read:	☐ all of it.	☐ most of it.	☐ parts of it.

Ferocious Dragons – 2

1. Which lines rhyme in each verse of *Ferocious Dragons*?

   (a) first and third ☐   (b) second and fourth ☐   (c) first and last ☐

2. Write a word from the poem that matches each definition.
   The verse in which it is found is in the brackets.

   (a) fierce and cruel (1) _____

   (b) causing feelings of horror (3) _____

   (c) to send or give out (4) _____

3. In verse 2, what do 'towering, terrifying animals' refer to?

   _____

4. What is the main idea of verse 5?

   _____

   _____

5. A simile compares one thing with another. Match these similes.

   Dragons have: (a)   wings like   •   • lizards

                    (b)   scales like •   • serpents

                    (c)   tails like   •   • bats

6. (a) Does the writer of the poem believe dragons are real? [Yes] [No]

   (b) Explain your answer. _____

   _____

   (c) What do you think about dragons? _____

   _____

   _____

7. Choose your favourite verse from the poem. Practise reading it out loud using expression in your voice and actions to match the words. Perform to a small group or the class.

My learning log	While doing these activities:		
	I found Q ____ easy.	I found Q ____ challenging.	I found Q ____ interesting.

Ferocious Dragons – 3

1. The word 'creature' is used in the poem. The syllables in 'creature' are crea/ture.

Divide these words into two syllables. Write the syllables beside each word.	Divide these words into three syllables. Write the syllables beside each word.
nature	furniture
future	departure
mixture	adventure
picture	signature

2. Read these sentences and fill in the missing '-ture' words.

   (a) My dad bought a new sofa in the _____ shop.

   (b) The talented artist drew an amazing _____ in his sketchpad.

   (c) The plane's _____ was delayed because of fog.

3. Find words in the poem that mean the same as the following.

   (a) release   _____   (b) live   _____

   (c) dull and colourless _____   (d) enormous _____

4. The words 'there'/'their'/'they're' are homophones. Write each one in a sentence. The sentence should have something to do with dragons.

   (a) there   _____

   (b) their   _____

   (c) they're _____

   (d) Write the correct words in this sentence. _____ parents are

        waiting over _____ and _____ not very happy.

5. The words 'breathe' and 'breath' are near-homophones. Write them in the correct sentences.

   (a) The dragon's _____ was extremely smelly.

   (b) A dragon can _____ fire out of its mouth.

My learning log	*Colour:*	I ⌐understand⌐ / ⌐need more practice on⌐ syllables. I ⌐can read⌐ / ⌐can't read⌐ words ending in '-ture'. I ⌐know⌐ / ⌐don't know⌐ the difference between *there/their/they're*.

Life Cycle of a Sunflower

Curriculum Links

Activity	Code	Objective	Outcome
Text	C3 C4	• Listen to and discuss a wide range of non-fiction • Read books that are structured in different ways and for a range of purposes	• Can understand a flow chart
Comprehension	C1 C5 C15 C16	• Retrieve and record information from non-fiction • Use dictionaries to check the meaning of words that they have read • Identify main ideas drawn from more than one paragraph and summarise these • Identify how structure and presentation contribute to meaning	• Can answer questions about a non-fiction text • Can use a dictionary to write definitions of words • Can summarise content of an explanation • Can explain why a flow chart helps understanding of life cycles
Word Reading	WR1	• Apply their growing knowledge of suffixes	• Can read words ending in '-sure' and '-tion'

Additional Teacher Information

Definition of Terms

Explanation

An explanation is a text written in the form of a detailed description, which outlines how something occurs, works or is made. Its purpose is to inform the reader.

Flow chart

A flow chart is a graphic organiser used to record information in a series of steps. This information is recorded in sequential order, with illustrations, diagrams, arrows or labels to order the events. Flow charts can be organised in a straight line, circle or zigzag.

Links to other Curriculum Areas

• Science – Identifying and describing the functions of different parts of flowering plants and their life cycle

Terminology for Pupils

explanation
flow chart
non-fiction
definition
suffix
syllable
synonym

Suggested Reading

• Link about the life cycles of flowering plants:
  <http://www.bbc.co.uk/bitesize/ks2/science/living_things/plant_lifecycles/read/1/>

• Time lapse photography of a sunflower growing:
  <https://www.youtube.com/watch?v=zst08tm9s6M>

• Time lapse photography of sunflowers following the sun:
  <https://www.youtube.com/watch?v=g8mr0R3ibPU>

• *From Seed to Sunflower* by **Legg Gerald**

• *The Lonely Sunflower* by **Julia Minigh**

Text

Teacher Information

- The flow chart on page 51 contains text and illustrations about the life cycle of a flowering plant—the sunflower. The arrows indicate the order to follow. If possible, display an actual sunflower for pupils to view or colour photographs. Pupils may like to grow sunflowers from seeds and monitor their progress.

Introduction

- Have a class discussion about sunflowers. Use visual aids to demonstrate and explain. Make out a class KWL (Know, Want to know, Learned) chart, leaving the 'L' column blank until after the reading.

Development

- Read and discuss the text with pupils, as a whole class or in groups. Assist pupils to decode new words if necessary. Discuss the meaning of any new or unfamiliar words and phrases. Question individual pupils to gauge their understanding of what they have listened to or read. Pupils should also ask questions about parts of the text they are unsure of, in order to improve their understanding of it.

- Have pupils focus on each individual paragraph of text. Ensure they understand the flow arrows. Ask pupils to come up with the main idea in each paragraph. Help them to see that putting all the main ideas together results in a summary of the text.

Differentiated Individual/Paired/Group Work

- Pupils should write a brief summary of the text, using the main ideas they identified in the class discussion. Ask them to illustrate any parts that would benefit from an illustration.

- Highly able readers should think about the main ideas they would include in an explanation about the life cycle of a frog/ butterfly. They could research this on the Internet, if necessary.

Review

- Recap the KWL chart created at the start of the lesson. Add in extra information into the 'K' and 'W' columns. Full attention should be devoted to completing the 'L' column.

Comprehension

Teacher Information

- Pupils will need a dictionary to complete question 1.

Introduction

- Revise and reread the explanation. Ask questions, such as: What is germination? What job does the root do? What does the leaf do? How tall can a sunflower grow? How does a sunflower make food? How can humans use sunflowers?

Development

- Discuss the structure of the text and how the flow chart assists the reader.

- Compare ideas for question 7 as there will be similarities and differences in their answers.

- Discuss the comprehension activities on page 52, before pupils complete the page independently.

Differentiated Individual/Paired/Group Work

Less Able Readers	Highly Able Readers
• Assist a small group of readers with decoding some of the more challenging words in this text. Encourage them to use any strategies to help them read the words. • Have pupils work in pairs to provide an oral summary of the main points in the life cycle of a sunflower.	• Have pupils research germination, photosynthesis and carbon dioxide. Have pupils give an oral retelling of their findings.

Review

- Pupils should read out their interesting facts about sunflowers.

- Ask pupils to create a list of questions to pose to other pupils in the class. Select some of the pupils to ask their questions to the class.

Word Reading

Teacher Information

- The activities on page 53 are designed to support the development of vocabulary with a variety of word reading exercises. They include working with words ending in '-sure' and '-tion' and unusual correspondences between spelling and sound. Words should be verbalised so pupils can hear the specific phoneme focused upon.

Introduction

- Have pupils silently reread the text. Ensure that pupils can read and understand any difficult words. This will help them when completing question 6.

Development

- Have pupils complete question 1 first, which asks them to find and underline any words ending in '-sure'. This question should be corrected before moving on to questions 2 and 3. Ensure pupils focus on the sound of '-sure' when reading the words.

- Once questions 2 and 3 are completed, have pupils work on question 4 to locate the '-tion' words in the text.

- Question 5 provides an opportunity for work on syllables with the '-tion' word ending. If time allows, do the same with the words in questions 1 and 2.

Differentiated Individual/Paired/Group Work

Less Able Readers	Highly Able Readers
• Work with a small group on the syllable division of words. Provide extra practice, particularly with any words that end in '-tion' or '-sure'.	• Ask pupils to try and place some of the '-tion' words in sentences. Challenge them to create sentences with 2, 3 or even 4 words in the same sentence. • Ask pupils to come up with a vocabulary quiz. Have them select 5-8 words from the text (and/or from the words ending in '-sure' and '-tion'). Ask them to compose questions/definitions with these words as the answers.

Review

- Bring the whole class together and sum up the things the class have learned. If some pupils created the vocabulary quiz questions, this would be an ideal time to group/pair pupils to let them answer the questions.

Assessment

C1	Ask the pupils to write their own non-fiction piece on 'Sunflowers'. They should write it in a question and answer format (for example, What happens to a sunflower seed?). If some pupils find this difficult, you can provide a structure/help, noting this as part of the assessment.
C15	Read another non-fiction piece (for example, *The Life Cycle of a Butterfly*). Ask pupils to write down the main ideas that this piece contains.
WR1	Ask the pupils to write words that could end in either '–sure' or '–tion' based on the following: Something a pirate hides: _____ Where a train pulls in: _____ A made-up story: _____ Weight or force: _____ Something newly created: _____ The answer to a problem: _____ Note the pupils who can identify and correctly spell each word. Did they use syllabification to help spell the words?

Answers

Comprehension

1. (a) substances necessary for life and growth
   (b) fine, yellowish powder
   (c) the plural of 'ovum' meaning 'egg'
   (d) removed or taken out
2. The flow chart has arrows which show the reader the correct order to follow in the life cycle.
3. (c), (d), (a), (b)
4. The seeds wouldn't germinate because they need warmth and dampness.
5. They both carry water and nutrients.
6. (a) Yes
   (b) The author says positive things about them such as 'lovely plants' and they look like they're smiling.
7. Teacher check

Word Reading

1. pleasure, measure
2. Teacher check
3. (a) pleasure   (b) treasure   (c) enclosure
   (d) pressure   (e) measure
4. explanation, germination, information
5. in/jec/tion, poll/u/tion, ac/tion, na/tion, in/ven/tion, sta/tion, fic/tion, sol/u/tion
6. (a) damp   (b) bright   (c) warm
   (d) smiling   (e) begins   (f) above

Life Cycle of a Sunflower – 1

Read the explanation in the flow chart.

Have you seen sunflowers growing in a garden? These lovely plants have large flower heads with bright yellow petals. It is a pleasure to look at sunflowers. Sunflowers look as if they are smiling at you! During growth, sunflowers tilt during the day to face the sun. Here is some information about their life cycle.

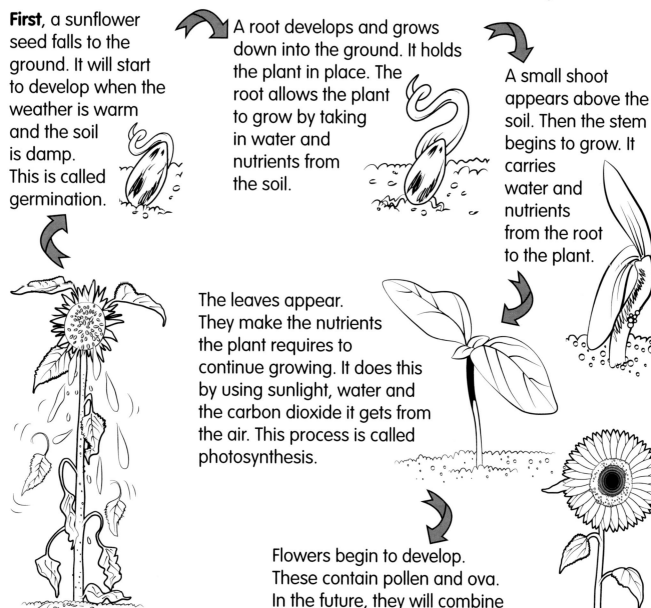

First, a sunflower seed falls to the ground. It will start to develop when the weather is warm and the soil is damp. This is called germination.

A root develops and grows down into the ground. It holds the plant in place. The root allows the plant to grow by taking in water and nutrients from the soil.

A small shoot appears above the soil. Then the stem begins to grow. It carries water and nutrients from the root to the plant.

The leaves appear. They make the nutrients the plant requires to continue growing. It does this by using sunlight, water and the carbon dioxide it gets from the air. This process is called photosynthesis.

Flowers begin to develop. These contain pollen and ova. In the future, they will combine to produce seeds which will eventually germinate and grow into new plants. Sunflowers are fully grown in about three months. If you need to measure them, they can grow up to three metres tall.

The petals and leaves fall off as the flowers die. Seeds will begin to form inside each flower.

Did you know that sunflower seeds are very good for you as they are full of nutrients such as Vitamin E? Oil is extracted from the seeds too and used in cooking. Have you tasted crunchy sunflower seeds?

My learning log	When I read this explanation, I could read:	☐ all of it.	☐ most of it.	☐ parts of it.

Life Cycle of a Sunflower – 2

1. Use a dictionary to write a definition for each word.

   (a) nutrients _____

   (b) pollen _____

   (c) ova _____

   (d) extracted _____

2. The author has used a flow chart as the main part of the explanation. How does this help the reader to understand the life cycle?

   _____

   _____

3. Number these parts of the life cycle in the correct order.

   (a) The leaves start growing. ☐   (b) The sunflower is fully grown. ☐

   (c) A seed germinates. ☐   (d) The root develops. ☐

4. What do you think would happen if you planted some sunflower seeds and the weather stayed cool and dry?

   _____

   _____

5. What is similar about a sunflower's roots and stem?

   _____

6. (a) Do you think the author likes sunflowers? [Yes] [No]

   (b) Explain your answer. _____

   _____

7. Write an interesting fact you learnt about sunflowers.

   _____

   _____

My learning log	While doing these activities:		
	I found Q _____ easy.	I found Q _____ challenging.	I found Q _____ interesting.

Life Cycle of a Sunflower – 3

1. Reread the explanation text and underline any words that end in '-sure'. Write them here.

   _____

2. Read these words that end in '-sure'.

   | treasure | pressure | pleasure | measure | enclosure |

3. Write the missing '-sure' words into these sentences.

   (a) It was a great _____ to help organise the birthday party.

   (b) The pirates found _____ on the deserted island.

   (c) The tigers were in a secure _____ at the zoo.

   (d) Dad checked the _____ of the car tyres.

   (e) Our teacher asked us to _____ the length of the piece of string.

4. Reread the explanation text and underline any words that end in '-tion'. Write them here.

   _____

5. Read these words that end in '-tion'. Divide them into syllables. Write the syllables beside the word.

injection	pollution
action	nation
invention	station
fiction	solution

6. Find a word from the text that is a synonym for these.

   (a) wet   _____   (b) dazzling _____

   (c) hot   _____   (d) grinning _____

   (e) starts   _____   (f) over   _____

My learning log	*Colour:*	I [can read] / [can't read] words ending in '-sure'.
		I [can read] / [can't read] words ending in '-tion'.
		I [know] / [don't know] the synonyms of the words on this page.

Curriculum Links

Activity	Code	Objective	Outcome
Text	C3 C6 C16	• Listen to and discuss a wide range of non-fiction • Increase their familiarity with a wide range of books • Identify how language, structure and presentation contribute to meaning	• Can read and discuss exposition texts
Comprehension	C1 C7 C11	• Retrieve and record information from non-fiction • Identify themes and conventions • Check that the text makes sense to them and discuss their understanding	• Can answer questions about an exposition • Can distinguish fact from opinion
Word Reading	WR1 WR2	• Apply their growing knowledge of root words • Read further exception words, noting the unusual correspondences between spelling and sound, and where these occur in the word	• Can read (and spell) some words with 'sc'

Additional Teacher Information

Definition of Terms

Exposition

An exposition is a persuasive text which argues for a particular position with the purpose of persuading the audience to share this view. An exposition may be written in the form of an essay, email, letter, policy statement, critical review, advertisement, editorial or speech.

Fact

Something that is true or real.

Opinion

A view or judgement formed about something, not necessarily based on fact or knowledge.

Links to other Curriculum Areas

• Art and design – Vincent Van Gogh

Terminology for Pupils

exposition
argument
paragraph
fact
opinion
exclamation mark
word
phrase
root word
sentence

Suggested Reading

• Camille and the Sunflowers: *A story about Vincent Van Gogh by Laurence Anholt* (Based on a real-life incident)

• *Van Gogh and the Sunflowers* by **Laurence Anholt**

Text

Teacher Information

- The text on page 57 is a persuasive text written in the form of an exposition. While the topic is not one concerning a serious issue, the writer has still used arguments for a clearly stated position to persuade the reader to share the view that yellow is the best colour. Controlling and emotive words are used such as 'You must agree', 'best', 'many' and the use of exclamation marks for emphasis. Each paragraph states and elaborates on each point or argument. Arguments are usually written from the strongest to the weakest. The final paragraph restates the writer's position.

Introduction

- Read and discuss the exposition with pupils, as a whole class or in groups. Assist pupils to decode new words if necessary. Ask the pupils what they think makes this passage easy to read. (Use of 'My' and 'I', ordinary language and words, no scientific terms, the exclamation marks, etc.)

Development

- Discuss the meaning of any new or unfamiliar words and phrases. Question individual pupils to gauge their understanding of what they have listened to or read. Pupils should also ask questions about parts of the exposition they are unsure of, in order to improve their understanding of it.

- Have pupils explore the structure of this text against a non-fiction text (Unit 8, *Life Cycle of a Sunflower*). Place particular emphasis on fact versus opinion. Ask pupils what sentences are opinion. Are there any facts? Was there any opinion in the *Life Cycle of a Sunflower* text?

Differentiated Individual/Paired/Group Work

- Pupils should note down any sentences where the author is giving his opinion. Do they agree or disagree? Ask them to create a list of some of the author's main reasons for saying that yellow is the best colour.

- Assign different groups a colour, and ask them to suggest reasons why it should be considered the best colour. Remind them to be aware of fact versus opinion. The group leader can write down the main points the group think of.

Review

- Ask each group to feed back to the whole class, saying what they have thought of. Have a class vote after each group has given their presentation. Which is the 'best' colour?

Comprehension

Teacher Information

- See *Teacher Information* in the *Text* column.

Introduction

- Ask pupils to reread the passage carefully.

- Ask quick questions such as: Why does the author say yellow is the happiest colour? Name some foods that are yellow. Where can yellow be seen in nature? What famous art work uses a lot of yellow?

Development

- Discuss the comprehension activities on page 58, before pupils complete the page independently. Discuss the structural and language features outlined in the *Teacher Information* section, under *Text*.

- Have the whole class come together to correct and discuss each question. In particular, compare their answers to questions 2 and 7 as answers may vary.

Differentiated Individual/Paired/Group Work

Less Able Readers	Highly Able Readers
• Give less confident writers a structure to base their writing on: _____ is an important colour because ………. Fruits such as …. are _____. • The colour _____ is used/can be seen in ……….	• Have pupils pick their favourite colour and write their own exposition, based on the text on page 57. Encourage pupils to give thoughtful opinions on the colour. They should be encouraged to try and pick reasons that will help readers agree with their point of view.

Review

- Invite some pupils to read out their favourite colour piece. Invite other pupils to comment on the opinions in the piece. Were they good opinions? Do these opinions help convince you to like that colour? When you were listening to the exposition, were there any ideas that you hadn't thought about before? Could you offer any other suggestion that the pupil could add in about his/her colour?

Word Reading

Teacher Information

- The activities on page 59 are designed to support the development of vocabulary with a variety of word reading exercises. They include identifying words built from root words, and distinguishing and identifying usual and unusual correspondences between spelling and sound and where they occur in a word. Words should be spoken out loud so pupils can hear the specific phoneme focused upon.

- Pupils may need a dictionary to complete question 5.

Introduction

- Reread the passage, telling the pupils that they will be focusing on root words.

Development

- Explore the roots of common words that the pupils are familiar with; e.g. laugh: laughing, laughed, laughs. Demonstrate how to examine a word to identify its root. Ask the pupils to notice what can be added to root words. Scribe these on the board for the pupils to refer to later.

- Have pupils complete questions 1 and 2 independently. Correct and discuss as a whole class. Refer back to the list the pupils made on the board about root words. Are there any other things they need to add to that list?

- Direct the pupils' attention to the last sentence in the first paragraph. Identify and write the word 'fascinated' on the board. Discuss the sound 'sc' makes. Make a list of the other words that the pupils will encounter in question 4 on the board (science, scene, crescent, discipline, scissors, descend, muscle, scent). Ensure pupils can read and decode these words. Draw attention to the 'sc' in each word.

- Have the pupils complete questions 3, 4 and 5 independently.

Differentiated Individual/Paired/Group Work

Less Able Readers	Highly Able Readers
• Provide extra practice for those pupils who are struggling with reading 'sc' words.	• Have highly able readers write their own sentences containing 'sc' words.

Review

- Play a sentence completion game. All the words should have 'sc' in them. Call out a sentence such as:
  - My favourite subject at school is _____.
  - Dad cut the fabric with a pair of _____.
  Pupils should write/call out the word.

Assessment

C11	Ask the pupils to demonstrate their understanding of fact versus opinion by asking them to write down one fact and one opinion of the following topics: Flowers Space Scotland Bananas
WR1	Challenge the pupils to reread the text, write down five words from the text and identify the root word from which they come.
WR2	Provide a grid such as the following and ask pupils to complete it: <table><tr><td>'sc' at the start of a word</td><td>'sc' in the middle of a word</td></tr><tr><td></td><td></td></tr></table>

Answers

Comprehension

1. To persuade readers that yellow is the best colour.
2. (a) Yellow is the happiest colour and makes you feel cheerful when wearing or looking at it.
   (b)–(c) Teacher check
3. bananas
4. The best breakfasts are made from yellow food.
5. They don't look yellow but are on the inside.
6. (a) Opinion   (b) Fact   (c) Opinion
7. They are used for emphasis and to try to persuade the reader to agree with the author.

Word Reading

1. (a) scrambled   (b) wearing   (c) welcoming
   (d) cheerful   (e) happiest   (f) beautiful
2. (a) scrambling   (b) welcomed   (c) happier
   (d) beautiful
3. sc
4. science, scene, crescent, discipline, scissors, descend, muscle, scent
5. (a) scene   (b) descend   (c) crescent
   (d) discipline   (e) scissors   (f) scent

Yellow is the Best Colour – 1

Read the exposition.

I think yellow is the best colour in the whole world. I like other colours too … but yellow is the best! I am fascinated by all things yellow.

You must agree that yellow is the happiest colour. I don't feel happy looking at or wearing dark colours. But yellow is so bright it makes me feel like smiling. When I wear or look at something yellow, I feel so happy and cheerful!

Yellow is an important colour. Our sun is yellow. Without the sun, Earth would have no light or warmth. That's another reason why yellow is the best colour.

Many delicious fruits and vegetables are yellow. Yellow fruits and vegetables have lots of Vitamin C. This helps to keep our body healthy.

My favourite yellow vegetable is corn. I love eating hot corn on the cob spread with yellow butter or margarine. It makes my mouth water when I see it being cooked!

Bananas, some apples and pears, and lemons are yellow fruits. Lemon meringue pie is my favourite dessert. It's filled with tangy lemon custard with a fluffy meringue topping. Delicious! My favourite fruit of all doesn't look yellow from the outside. But what a surprise when you cut it open—delicious, juicy, yellow chunks of pineapple are inside!

The best breakfasts are made from yellow food. Can you guess what food it is? Yes, eggs! I like the yellow yolks a bit runny when I have hard-boiled eggs. That means you can dip toast fingers into the slightly gooey yolks. I also love fluffy, yellow omelettes and scrambled eggs on toast.

My two favourite flowers are yellow and grow in our garden. Beautiful yellow daffodils bloom in the spring. Our garden looks so welcoming with our friendly sunflowers. Their large, round, yellow faces look as if they're smiling at you! We have a copy of a well-known sunflower painting hanging in our hallway. It was painted by Vincent Van Gogh, a famous Dutch artist. He rented a yellow house in France in which to paint his sunflowers. What a great idea!

You must agree with me that yellow is the best colour of all. There's no other colour that always makes me— and many other people—feel so joyous!

My learning log	When I read this exposition, I could read:	☐ all of it.	☐ most of it.	☐ parts of it.

1. Why did the author write this text?

   _____

2. (a) An author includes several arguments in an exposition to try to persuade the reader. The strongest argument is usually stated first. Summarise this argument.

   _____

   _____

   (b) Do you think this is the strongest argument?   Yes   No

   (c) If not, which argument do you think is the strongest?

   _____

   _____

3. Of these fruits, circle the one the author would most likely want to eat.

   | cherries | plums | strawberries | bananas | oranges |

4. What is the main idea of the seventh paragraph?

   _____

5. Why does the author think pineapples are surprising?

   _____

6. Write 'Fact' or 'Opinion'.

   (a) Yellow is the best colour.   _____

   (b) Egg yolks are yellow.   _____

   (c) Yellow makes people feel cheerful. _____

7. Why do you think the author has used exclamation marks, and words and phrases like 'best' and 'you must agree' in the text?

   _____

   _____

My learning log	While doing these activities:		
	I found Q _____ easy.	I found Q _____ challenging.	I found Q _____ interesting.

Yellow is the Best Colour – 3

1. Write a word from the text built from these root words.

   (a) scramble _____   (b) wear _____

   (c) welcome _____   (d) cheer _____

   (e) happy _____   (f) beauty _____

2. Change these root words to fit in the sentence.

   (a) Mum is (scramble) _____ the eggs for breakfast.

   (b) The manager (welcome) _____ the customer into the shop.

   (c) I was (happy) _____ than my friend when I saw the cake.

   (d) The little boy had a (beauty) _____ smile.

3. In the sentence 'I am fascinated by all things yellow', the word 'fascinated' has an 's' sound.

   Write the two letters that make this sound. _____

4. Here are other words that have the same letters making the 's' sound. Underline the letters in each one.

science	scene	crescent	discipline
scissors	descend	muscle	scent

5. Write the words from question 4 beside the meaning.

   (a) place where an event happens _____

   (b) to go down _____

   (c) shaped like the new moon _____

   (d) order and rules _____

   (e) tool used for cutting _____

   (f) a smell, odour or fragrance _____

My learning log	*Colour:*	I [can change] / [can't change] root words.
		I [know] / [don't know] the meaning of the words *crescent*, *scene* and *descend*.
		I [can read] / [can't read] words with the 'sc' sound.

Curriculum Links

Activity	Code	Objective	Outcome
Text	C2 C3 C6	• Participate in discussions, taking turns and listening to what others say • Listen to and discuss a wide range of fiction • Increase their familiarity with a wide range of books	• Can engage in a class discussion on folk tales
Comprehension	C5 C7 C14	• Use dictionaries to check the meaning of words they have read • Identify themes and conventions • Predict what might happen from details stated and implied	• Can see similarities and differences between two folk tales
Word Reading	WR1	• Apply their growing knowledge of root words, prefixes and suffixes	• Can apply rules for prefixes and suffixes

Additional Teacher Information

Definition of Terms

Narrative

A narrative is a text that tells a story. It includes a title, an orientation (setting, time and characters), a complication to the main character(s), a series of events, a resolution to the complication and an ending.

Folk tale

A folk tale is a form of narrative, often set in the distant past. They are stories which have been passed from one generation to the next, often originally by word of mouth rather than being written down. Folk tales may include sayings, superstitions, social rituals, legends or lore about the weather, animals or plants.

Paragraph

A distinct section of a piece of writing, usually dealing with a single theme and indicated by a new line, indentation or numbering.

Terminology for Pupils

folk tale
version
root word
suffix
adverb
antonym
prefix

Suggested Reading

An online version can be found at:

<http://www.dltk-teach.com/fables/stonesoup/mtale.htm>

• *Stone Soup* by **Marcia Brown**
• *Stone Soup* by **Leslie Sims**
• *Nail Soup* by **Eric Maddern**

Links to other Curriculum Areas

• PSHE – Personal, social, health and economic education

Text

Teacher Information

- The folk tales on page 63 are based on *Stone Soup*, an old folk tale of which there are several versions from various European countries such as Sweden, Hungary, France, Russia, Germany and Ireland. The basic storyline is that a traveller, or travellers, arrive at a village/cottage (or similar) empty handed. The villagers do not want to part with food as it is scarce. The travellers trick the villagers into putting ingredients into a cooking pot, thereby making 'stone' soup. The moral behind the tale is that if we cooperate and pool resources we can accomplish more. The story is most commonly known as *Stone Soup*. Other titles include *Nail Soup*, *Axe Soup*, *Wood Soup*, *Button Soup* and *A Pot of Broth*.

Introduction

- Ask pupils if they have read any folk tales, or know of any folk tales. Discuss what they think the features of a folk tale are. Read and discuss the folk tales with pupils, as a whole class or in groups. Assist pupils to decode new words if necessary. Discuss the meaning of any new or unfamiliar words and phrases.

Development

- Question individual pupils to gauge their understanding of what they have listened to or read. Pupils should also ask questions about parts of the text they are unsure of, in order to improve their understanding of it. In the discussion, have pupils think about how the two versions are similar, and how they differ. Scribe these on the board. Ask pupils to consider the characters in the folk tales. What kind of person was the traveller? The old woman? Encourage them to use evidence from the folk tales to support their opinions.

Differentiated Individual/Paired/Group Work

- Pupils should retell the story to a partner. One pupil retells *Stone Soup*, while the partner retells *Nail Soup*.

- Have highly able readers compose their own folk tale on *A Pot of Broth* and ask them to be as creative as possible. Less confident readers might do the same activity but in a small group with the teacher acting as scribe.

Review

- Bring the class together and ask selected groups/individuals to read/tell their folk tale.

Comprehension

Teacher Information

- Pupils will need a dictionary for question 2.

Introduction

- Ask the pupils to reread both folk tales. Ask some quick recap questions on the story to ensure they know the details.

Development

- Talk about the similarities and differences between the stories and discuss that these are features of folk tales handed down over time and from different countries. Have pupils underline similarities in one colour, and differences in another colour. This will help them when attempting question 1.

- Compare answers to questions 3, 4 and 5 as they may vary. Pupils need to justify a 'Yes' or 'No' answer to questions 3 and 4. They are more likely to say 'Yes' to both but can be correct if they justify a 'No' answer.

- Discuss the comprehension activities on page 64, before pupils complete the page independently.

Differentiated Individual/Paired/Group Work

Less Able Readers	Highly Able Readers
• Work with a small group and focus on some of the more challenging words in this passage – their decoding and meaning (e.g. enormous, welcoming, scarce, smooth, ingredients, suspiciously). Help them practise essential dictionary skills while doing this activity.	• Ask pupils to write a short summary of one of the folk tales. Have them write each main point of the summary on a separate line. When finished, ask them to cut the sentences into strips. Give these strips to another pupil to sequence in the correct order. When correctly done, the pupil can stick them in the correct order onto a page.

Review

- Ask pupils to sum up the similarities and differences they noticed in the two folk tales.

Word Reading

Teacher Information

- The activities on page 65 are designed to support the development of vocabulary with a variety of word reading exercises. They include identifying suffixes and prefixes to add to root words and exploring antonyms.

- Words should be spoken out loud so pupils can hear the specific phoneme focused upon.

Introduction

- Play a synonym game with the class. Ask them to use the text to underline a word that means the same as: 1. huge, 2. small town, 3. not rough, 4. tasty, 5. quickly, 6. full of nutrients, 7. tired and exhausted, 8. came towards, 9. showing no trust, 10. commented or said.

Development

- Explore the use of suffixes. Ask pupils to identify any suffixes in the story. Remind pupils about the term 'root word'.

- Have pupils complete questions 1 and 2 independently.

- Discuss antonyms. Elicit from pupils antonyms to words they have already discussed in class (common ones include clean/dirty, high/low, hard/soft, right/left/wrong, deep/shallow, damp/dry). Ask pupils to complete question 3.

- Discuss prefixes. Compare with suffixes. Focus on the prefixes 'un-', 'dis-' and 'mis-' and how they create the opposites of words. Have pupils attempt questions 4 and 5.

Differentiated Individual/Paired/Group Work

Less Able Readers	Highly Able Readers
• Provide more practice for pupils on both suffixes and prefixes. Some pupils might benefit from lists for each prefix/suffix, which they can keep in a folder.	• Have highly able readers write sentences and, underneath in a different colour, have them change the sentence to the opposite. Encourage them to use the prefixes 'mis-', 'dis-' and 'un-'.

Review

- Play a quick word game. Say a word and pupils must either give its synonym or its antonym. Have pupils think of the words that are used.

Assessment

C6	Without looking at the folk tale, ask pupils to write their own folk tale with the title 'The Mysterious Visitor'. Ask them to plan out the setting, the characters and the plot. This will take several lessons.
WR1	Create a grid such as the following and ask pupils to fill it in, using either prefixes or suffixes. Pick words that your class have encountered before.

	usual	behave	honest
prefix	unusual	misbehave	dishonest
suffix	usually	behaving	honesty

Answers

Comprehension

1. Teacher check
2. (a) not enough, insufficient
   (b) moved back or withdrew
   (c) add to or decorate, especially food
3. Pupils will most likely agree that the travellers were clever because the travellers got the villagers/old woman to part with their precious supplies, without realising what the travellers were really up to. A negative answer needs to be justified.
4. Pupils will most likely agree that the travellers will make soup again as both travellers took the stone or nail with them, most likely to use again. A negative answer needs to be justified.
5. Teacher check

Word Reading

1. (a) traveller (b) fetched (c) wonderful
   (d) welcoming
2. (a) hastily (b) suspiciously (c) thoroughly
3. (a) smooth (b) scarce (c) hastily
   (d) long
4. (a) unwilling (b) unequal (c) ungrateful
   (d) unusual
5. mis-: behave, lead, understand, spell, treat
   dis-: agree, honest, appear, believe, obey

Stone Soup and Nail Soup – 1

Read the two versions of a folk tale.

Stone Soup

One day, a cold, tired and hungry traveller carrying an enormous cooking pot arrived at a small village. Instead of welcoming the stranger, the villagers retreated into their homes as they were unwilling to share what little food supplies they had left. Food was scarce at the end of a long winter.

The traveller called out that he wanted to make stone soup and share it with all of them. He filled the pot with water and built a fire under it. Then he took a smooth stone from his pocket and dropped it into the pot.

The villagers watched the stone soup bubble away in the pot. The thought of a delicious soup made them come out of their homes. One by one they sniffed the soup. The traveller said it was wonderful but would be better if it had some garnish like salt and some carrots. Two villagers hastily went and fetched some. Other villagers said they might be able to find other ingredients to put in the soup. So onions, cabbage, salted beef and potatoes were added. The nourishing soup was thoroughly enjoyed by all.

The next day the satisfied traveller went on his way, carrying the pot and stone.

Nail Soup

Once there was a cold, hungry, weary traveller who was walking through a thick forest. As he passed through a clearing, he spotted a small cottage with smoke rising from the chimney. He approached the front door and knocked softly. An old woman opened it and looked at him suspiciously. She thought he was going to ask for food and she had little left at the end of a long winter. However, the traveller asked if he could sleep in her barn for the night and, in return, he would make her nail soup.

She looked at him for a while and then replied that that would be lovely as she didn't have much food to share. She fetched a large pot of water and heated it over the cosy fire. The traveller got a rusty nail from his pocket and dropped it into the pot. He tasted the liquid and decided it needed some salt. The woman fetched him some. He tasted it again and remarked it would be tastier if it had some vegetables. The woman checked what she had left and gave him onions, carrots and cabbage. Now the soup smelt and tasted delicious. The two of them each ate a large bowl.

The next day, the traveller fished his nail out from the leftover soup and went on his way.

My learning log	When I read this folk tale, I could read:	☐ all of it. ☐ most of it. ☐ parts of it.

Stone Soup and Nail Soup – 2

1. *Stone Soup* and *Nail Soup* are two versions of a folk tale. There are similarities and differences between the tales. Complete the table below.

	Stone Soup	Nail Soup
(a) Describe the main character		
(b) Describe the setting		
(c) Who was the soup made for?		
(d) Ingredients used		
(e) Words used to describe the soup		
(f) Conclusion		

2. Use a dictionary to write the meaning of these words.

    (a) scarce _____

    (b) retreated _____

    (c) garnish _____

3. (a) Do you think the travellers were clever? ☐ Yes ☐ No

    (b) Explain your answer. _____

    _____

    _____

4. (a) Do you think each traveller will make soup again? ☐ Yes ☐ No

    (b) Why do you think this? _____

    _____

5. Think of another ingredient that could be used to start the soup instead of a stone or nail.

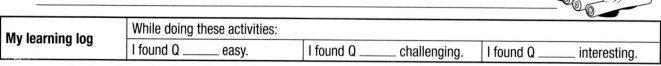

_____

My learning log	While doing these activities:		
	I found Q _____ easy.	I found Q _____ challenging.	I found Q _____ interesting.

Stone Soup and Nail Soup – 3

1. Add one of the these suffixes to each root word to make words in the text. (Check the spelling in the text.)

-er	-ing	-ed	-ful

   (a) travel _____

   (b) fetch _____

   (c) wonder _____

   (d) welcome _____

2. Add the suffix '-ly' to these root words to make adverbs used in the text that showed how things were done. (Check the spelling in the text.)

   (a) haste   Two villagers _____ fetched some garnishes.

   (b) suspicious   The old woman looked _____ at him.

   (c) thorough   The tasty soup was _____ enjoyed by all.

3. Find the antonyms of these words in the text.

   (a) rough _____

   (b) plentiful _____

   (c) slowly _____

   (d) short _____

4. The prefix 'un-' can be added to some words to make the opposite. Write the antonyms of these words.

   (a) willing _____

   (b) equal _____

   (c) grateful _____

   (d) usual _____

5. The prefixes 'mis-' and 'dis-' can also make the antonyms of some words. Which words need 'mis-' and which words need 'dis-'?

agree	behave	lead	understand	honest
appear	spell	treat	believe	obey

mis-	dis-

My learning log	*Colour:*	I ⌐understand⌐ / ⌐need more practice on⌐ antonyms.
		I ⌐know⌐ / ⌐don't know⌐ how to use the prefix 'un-'.
		I ⌐know⌐ / ⌐don't know⌐ how to use the prefixes 'dis-' and 'mis-'.

The Stone Age

Curriculum Links

Activity	Code	Objective	Outcome
Text	C3 C12 C15	• Listen to and discuss a wide range of non-fiction • Ask questions to improve their understanding of a text • Identify main ideas drawn from more than one paragraph and summarise these	• Can ask and answer questions about a non-fiction text
Comprehension	C1 C5 C11	• Retrieve and record information from non-fiction • Use dictionaries to check the meaning of words that they have read • Check that the text makes sense to them, discussing their understanding and explaining the meaning of words in context	• Can use non-fiction texts to generate information
Word Reading	WR1 WR2	• Apply their growing knowledge of root words and suffixes • Read further exception words, noting the unusual correspondences between spelling and sound	• Can recognise and apply suffixes • Can recognise and distinguish between homographs

Additional Teacher Information

Definition of Terms

Report

Reports are written documents describing the findings of an individual or group about a specific subject.

Explanation

An explanation is a text written in the form of a detailed description, which outlines how something occurs, works or is made. Its purpose is to inform the reader.

Heading

A heading tells the reader what a section of a text is about. It guides the reader through the text by showing the main idea of the sections being read. A heading is usually larger than the body text and is often in bold print.

Homograph

Two words are homographs if they look exactly the same when written but have different meanings. They may be pronounced differently.

Links to other Curriculum Areas

• History – Changes in Britain during the Stone Age

Terminology for Pupils

report
explanation
word
paragraph
heading
suffix
root word
homograph
definition

Suggested Reading

• Series of several short stories: *Littlenose the Neanderthal* by **John Grant**
• Step Into: *The Stone Age* by **Charlotte Hurdman**
• *The Savage Stone Age* (Horrible Histories) by **Terry Deary**
• Stone Age, Bone Age: *A Book About Prehistoric People* by **Mick Manning**

Text

Teacher Information

- The text on page 69 is a report on what is meant by the 'Stone Age', changes that occurred during that time and how flint tools were used.

Introduction

- If possible, find colour images of scenes from this era and pictures of flint tools. There are many images on the Internet. Discuss the features of these images and relate them to topics studied in history.

- Read and discuss the text with pupils, as a whole class or in groups. Assist pupils to decode new words if necessary. Pay particular attention to words such as 'flint', 'overhang', 'cereals', 'knapped' and 'chiselling'.

Development

- Discuss the meaning of any new or unfamiliar words and phrases. Question individual pupils to gauge their understanding of what they have listened to or read.

- Pupils should also ask questions about parts of the text they are unsure of, in order to improve their understanding of it. Ask if they know whether this is fiction or non-fiction. How do they know? What are the features of the text that are typical of non-fiction?

- Go through each paragraph and discuss with the pupils ways to decide upon the main idea(s) of each one.

Differentiated Individual/Paired/Group Work

- Have pupils summarise the main points from this text.

- Based on the details of the text, ask pupils to draw a labelled picture of a typical Stone Age scene. Ask them to include as many details as mentioned in the text.

- Ask highly able readers to write down the changes that occurred in the Stone Age.

Review

- Sum up any common features of non-fiction texts. Ask the pupils to give a quick synopsis of the text.

Comprehension

Introduction

- Reread the report and ask pupils some recap questions on the content.

- Pupils might need a dictionary to complete question 1.

Development

- Discuss the structure of the text, how the heading questions clarify the main idea of the paragraphs below and how the numbered steps also assist the reader.

- Discuss the comprehension activities on page 70, before pupils complete the page independently.

- Compare their answers to question 7 as answers will vary.

Differentiated Individual/Paired/Group Work

Less Able Readers	Highly Able Readers
• Help a group of less able readers come up with a way of extracting and recording information from a non-fiction piece. A template with headings or questions can be helpful. In this case, helpful questions might include: What was the Stone Age? When was the Stone Age? What did people do? What did they eat? How did they live? How did they make tools?	• Have highly able readers use the information in the text to help them write a fiction piece about 'A day in the life of a child living in the Stone Age'. Encourage them to keep it consistent with the facts of the time.

Review

- Bring the whole class back together and ask pupils to sum up the most important things they have learned. Ask what questions would be important, to find out information, if they were learning about the Iron Age or the Bronze Age.

Word Reading

Teacher Information

- The activities on page 71 are designed to support the development of vocabulary with a variety of word reading exercises. They include sorting words into groups, identifying the correct suffixes to add to root words and homographs.
- Words should be verbalised so pupils can hear the specific phoneme focused upon.

Introduction

- Have pupils reread the text and ask them to underline any animals mentioned. This will help them with part of question 1, but will also give them a focused purpose for rereading the text.

Development

- Pupils should complete all of question 1 independently.
- Revise suffixes and root words with the pupils. Talk about the common suffixes added to words. Focus on words which double the final letter when the suffixes are added to them. Pupils should then complete questions 2 and 3.
- Questions 4 and 5 are on words with more than one meaning. To explain and demonstrate this, use example words such as park, match, wave, ring, duck, bat. Have pupils complete questions 4 and 5 independently.

Differentiated Individual/Paired/Group Work

Less Able Readers	Highly Able Readers
• Help pupils create a visual reminder to help distinguish the meanings of the words: rock, match, wave, ring, duck, bat • Have the pupils write these words into simple sentences which show the differences.	• Challenge highly able readers to distinguish the two meanings of the following words, pictorially, in sentences and in definitions: desert, project, refuse, present, conduct, sewer

Review

- Invite some pupils to read out the meanings they have found for the homographs.

Assessment

C15	Ask pupils to write down the main ideas from a topic in history that was covered recently (they can use *The Stone Age* text, if they choose). Ensure that the ideas written down correspond to the main details and not smaller, less important details. Note this in the assessment.
WR1	Provide pupils with a list of words which require a double letter when adding the suffix. Ask the pupils to change the word accordingly to add a range of suffixes. Words could include: hop + ed, begin + ing, sad + en, forgot + en, drum + er, prefer + ed, refer + ing, travel + er

Answers

Comprehension

1. (a) hides   (b) chiselling   (c) shafts
2. (a) True
   (b) It started 2.5 million years ago and ended 5000 years ago and that is a very long time.
3. (a) To describe what life was like at the beginning of the Stone Age.
   (b) To describe what life was like later in the Stone Age.
4. Flint had very sharp edges when split.
5. (a) beginning   (b) later
   (c) later   (d) beginning
6. They give the main idea of the paragraphs under the heading which helps the reader to understand.
7. Teacher check

Word Reading

1. Animals: sheep, cows, pigs, horses, goats
   Materials: stone, wood, clay, straw, sand, flint, metal, bronze, animal bone, skin, branch, rock, antler
   Foods: fruit, nuts, eggs, roots, shells, fish, wild animals, cereals, milk
   Tools: hand axes, spears, arrows, hammer
2. (a) commonly   (b) chiselling   (c) discovered
   (d) explanation   (e) later   (f) wooden
3. (a) shopping   (b) forgotten
   (c) beginner, swimming
4. (a) part of a body   (b) to remove the skin
5. (a) a large stone   (b) to sway from side to side

The Stone Age – 1

Read the report.

What is the Stone Age?

The Stone Age refers to the period of time when people used stone for making tools. Flint was commonly used as it has very sharp edges when split. The Stone Age began about 2.5 million years ago and ended approximately 5000 years ago when people started working with metal like bronze to make tools and other objects.

At the beginning of the Stone Age, people lived a hunter-gatherer way of life. This means they gathered food like fruit, nuts, eggs, roots and shells; hunted wild animals and caught fish. People moved from place to place to find food. They lived in caves, under rock overhangs or out in the open with shelters made from material like animal bones and skins or branches.

As time went by, people became farmers as they discovered how to grow crops like cereals and keep animals such as sheep, cows, pigs, horses and goats for food, milk and transport. They started to settle in small villages and built homes from materials like stone, wood, clay, straw and sand.

What are some ways Stone Age people used flint tools?

Stone Age people used tools like hand axes to skin animals they had killed, scrape the hides to be used for making clothes and shelters, and chop up meat and other food. Flint was used to produce sparks for making fire. Other tools were used to make shafts for spears and tips for arrows. This is an explanation of how an early flint hand axe was made.

1. A large piece of flint was collected.

2. The flint was knapped (shaped by chipping) with a rock called a hammerstone.

3. The edge was sharpened using a hammer made from stone, wood or antler.

4. The edge was trimmed by chiselling off tiny flakes with a pointed tool.

5. Finished hand axe.

Front view   Side view

As you can see in the illustration, early hand axes did not have a handle. Hand axes were later attached to wooden shafts.

My learning log	When I read this report, I could read:	☐ all of it. ☐ most of it. ☐ parts of it.

1. Find a word in the text to match each definition.

   (a) pelts or skins of large animals _____

   (b) carving out with a pointed object _____

   (c) long poles attached to devices like hammer heads _____

2. (a) The Stone Age lasted a long time. ⟨ True ⟩ ⟨ False ⟩

   (b) Explain your answer. _____

   _____

3. What is the main idea of:

   (a) Paragraph 2? _____

   _____

   (b) Paragraph 3? _____

   _____

4. Why was flint generally used to make tools?

   _____

5. Circle if these things happened at the beginning or later during the Stone Age.

   (a) living in caves ⟨ beginning   later ⟩

   (b) planting crops ⟨ beginning   later ⟩

   (c) holding an axe with a handle ⟨ beginning   later ⟩

   (d) living a hunter-gatherer life ⟨ beginning   later ⟩

6. Why have heading questions been used to present the information?

   _____

7. If you lived during the Stone Age, what job would you most like to do?

   _____

My learning log	While doing these activities:		
	I found Q _____ easy.	I found Q _____ challenging.	I found Q _____ interesting.

The Stone Age – 3

1. Find words in the report that can be put into the following word groups.

animals	materials
foods	**tools**

2. Add one of these suffixes to the root word to make words from the text. (Check the spelling in the text.)

-ly	-en	-ing	-er	-tion	-ed

(a) common _____ (b) chisel _____

(c) discover _____ (d) explain _____

(e) late _____ (f) wood _____

3. Some root words need to double the final letter before a suffix is added on. Write the following.

(a) I went (shop + ing) _____ for new shoes.

(b) Gran had (forgot + en) _____ where she left her glasses.

(c) My little sister is only at the (begin + er) _____ level in

(swim + ing) _____ class.

4. In the text, the word 'skin' has two meanings. Give a definition for each.

(a) skin (noun) _____

(b) skin (verb) _____

5. The word 'rock' also has two meanings. Give a definition for each.

(a) rock (noun) _____ (b) rock (verb) _____

My learning log	Write **Yes** or **No**.
	I know how to sort words into word groups. ☐
	I know when to double the final letter of a root word before I add a suffix. ☐
	I know that some words can be a verb and a noun. ☐

A Day at Skara Brae

Curriculum Links

Activity	Code	Objective	Outcome
Text	C3 C4	• Listen to and discuss a wide range of non-fiction • Read books that are structured in different ways and read for a range of purposes	• Can read and understand a diary entry
Comprehension	C1 C5 C13	• Retrieve and record information from non-fiction • Use dictionaries to check the meaning of words that they have read • Draw inferences and justify them with evidence	• Can answer questions about a diary • Can use a dictionary • Can infer from details stated and implied
Word Reading	WR1 WR2	• Apply their growing knowledge of root words • Read further exception words, noting the unusual correspondences between spelling and sound	• Can identify the root of words • Can spell common words with 'ch' pronounced /sh/

Additional Teacher Information

Definition of Terms

Diary entry
A personal record of daily events, appointments or observations.

Report
Reports are written documents describing the findings of an individual or group about a specific subject.

Links to other Curriculum Areas

• History – Changes in Britain from the Stone Age to the Iron Age. Late Neolithic hunter-gatherers and early farmers at Skara Brae.

Terminology for Pupils

diary
definition
synonym
antonym
root word
sentence

Suggested Reading

• This website shows videos and running commentary suitable for pupils. It is presented in cartoon form:
<http://www.bbc.co.uk/scotland/learning/primary/skarabrae/content/what_happened/>

• This website shows videos and written information about Skara Brae: <http://www.orkney.com/skara-brae>

• *Stone Age Farmers Beside the Sea* by **Caroline Arnold**

Text

Teacher Information

- The informative text about Skara Brae on page 75 has a short introduction with facts about the place, followed by an imaginary diary written by a child who lived there, which reveals insights about what life could have been like at the time. There are many images of Skara Brae on the Internet which would be useful for pupils to view while completing this unit. The diary entry has been written based on information that archaeologists have discovered about the well-preserved ruins of Skara Brae, some of which are still not fully substantiated.

Introduction

- Read and discuss the text with pupils, as a whole class or in groups. Assist pupils to decode new words if necessary.

Development

- Discuss the meaning of any new or unfamiliar words and phrases. Question individual pupils to gauge their understanding of of what they have listened to or read. Pupils should also ask questions about parts of the text they are unsure of, in order to improve their understanding of it.

- Discuss the features of diary entry writing with the pupils. Ask the pupils to identify any features which make this style different from non-fiction.

Differentiated Individual/Paired/Group Work

- Have pupils write a diary entry for today and include all the activities they have completed.

- Highly able readers could be challenged to write a diary entry, pretending they are someone from a historical period that has recently been studied in class.

Review

- Ask the class to recap the essential features of diary entries and select a few volunteers to briefly outline their diary entries with the class.

Comprehension

Teacher Information

- See information under *Teacher Information* in the *Text* column.
- Pupils might need a dictionary to complete question 3.

Introduction

- Reread the diary entry. Ask recap question such as: What is Skara Brae? Where is it located? What did people do there? What did they eat?

Development

- Discuss the comprehension activities on page 76, before pupils complete the page independently.

Differentiated Individual/Paired/Group Work

Less Able Readers	Highly Able Readers
• Work with a group of less able readers to understand the dictionary terms they searched for. Use these in sentences and then have the pupils illustrate them.	• In groups, highly able readers could imagine what it would be like for a child from Skara Brae if they could time travel and arrived in our time. What would they note in their diary entry? What would be the things that would amaze him/her most? What would be the things that he/she would miss most? Each group could work together to create the ideas and then write an individual piece on the topic.

Review

- Invite the class to listen to the accounts written by different pupils and have pupils discuss and comment on the ideas.

Word Reading

Teacher Information

- The activities on page 77 are designed to support the development of vocabulary with a variety of word reading exercises. They include synonyms, antonyms, identifying root words and reading 'ch' in certain words to sound like 'sh'. Words should be verbalised so pupils can hear the specific phoneme focused upon.

Introduction

- Have pupils read question 1 and question 2 first before they reread the text. Then allow them to reread and underline as they read. They can then fill in the correct answers independently.

Development

- Revise and develop work covered on root words. Make a list of the different changes that can happen to root words. Have pupils generate their own examples and scribe these on the board. Once all pupils are confident that they can recognise the root of a word, ask the pupils to complete question 3.

- Questions 4 and 5 provide practice on the 'ch' in words that sound like 'sh'. Write these words on the board or on a chart: machine, chef, brochure, chalet, parachute, quiche. Ensure pupils can read the words and draw attention to the 'ch'. Explain that these words are French in origin which explains the different sound attached to the 'ch'.

Differentiated Individual/Paired/Group Work

Less Able Readers	Highly Able Readers
• Have less able readers find the following words and use their dictionaries to find the meaning: heather, scooped, ornaments, precious, display, archaeologists	• Ask highly able readers to write an account on a day in the life of a famous archaeologist. They could research Howard Carter and use the information they find about the work of an archaeologist to help them write their account.

Review

- Ask some pupils to read out their account of 'A day in the life of a famous archaeologist'.

Assessment

C4	Ask pupils to write a diary entry on the following topic: 'My First Day in my New Year 3 Classroom'.
WR2	Provide pupils with a list of words (ensure the words are pairs of synonyms and pairs of antonyms). Present these words out of order and ask the pupils to pair them under the headings synonyms and antonyms. The list of words could include: west, calm, fresh, chores, largest, strong, east, wild, tasks, powerful, real, stale, precious, biggest, imaginary, valuable

Answers

Comprehension

1. In 1850 there was a storm that caused a section of land to be stripped away, revealing the ruins.
2. The buildings and contents were very well-preserved.
3. (a) grass and surface layer of earth held together by roots
   (b) a sea creature with a shell
   (c) the floor of a fireplace
4. Light from fireplace
5.

Fire	seaweed sheep and cow dung heather bracken flint
Clothing	deer skin
Mattress/Bed	heather straw
Insulation	food leftovers straw
Fishing/Bait	limpets fish traps

Word Reading

1. (a) battered   (b) wild
   (c) combination   (d) imaginary
2. (a) freezing   (b) fresh
   (c) live   (d) caught
3. (a) strip   (b) imagine   (c) activity
   (d) large   (e) extreme   (f) cause
   (g) complete (h) nice
4. Teacher check
5. (a) chef, quiche   (b) brochure   (c) parachute
   (d) machine   (e) chalet

A Day at Skara Brae – 1

Read the diary entry.

Skara Brae is a place on the west coast of Mainland, the largest island in the Orkney Islands, north of mainland Scotland. In 1850, a wild storm battered Orkney. A combination of extremely strong winds and very high tides caused a large section of turf and sand to be stripped away. This revealed the well-preserved ruins of ancient stone buildings and their contents. It was discovered that Skara Brae, as it is now known, had been built more than 5000 years ago in the late Stone Age. Archaeologists have learnt a lot about what life was like for the people who once lived there from studying the ruins. This is an imaginary diary entry from a child.

Dear Diary

I'm sure I'll sleep well tonight after completing so many chores today. The warm, fine July weather meant we could do more activities outside.

First we collected the leftovers from last night and this morning's meals to put in the middens between the walls of our houses. This helps to keep out the cold air, especially during our freezing winters.

Next we gathered fresh heather to put in the mattresses. Sometimes we use straw but heather has a nicer smell. The old filling was put in the middens.

Today was a good day to go fishing. We scooped some live limpets out of the tanks we keep inside and fetched some fish traps. The limpets have already had their shells removed. They are put in the traps and fish are caught when they go in to eat the limpets. While the traps were out, we searched for more limpets on the rocky shore. We also collected seaweed. This will be mixed with our sheep's and cows' dung along with heather and bracken, then used as fuel to add to the hearths in our houses.

At the moment, I'm lying on the bed I share with my sisters, looking at the lovely ornaments on our dresser. Every house has a stone dresser which displays precious things they've made. I can see Mum and my older sister working on a deer skin by the firelight. This will be made into clothing.

I'm going to sleep now. Tomorrow we'll be walking along the coast to collect more flint with which to make stone tools and to use to light our fires.

My learning log	When I read this diary entry, I could read:	☐ all of it. ☐ most of it. ☐ parts of it.

1. What caused the ruins of Skara Brae to be discovered?

_____

_____

2. How have archaeologists been able to learn what life was like at Skara Brae thousands of years ago?

_____

_____

3. Use a dictionary to write a definition for these words.

(a) turf _____

(b) limpet _____

(c) hearth _____

4. There was no electricity for light 5000 years ago. What do you think the people used for light at night or on dark days?

_____

5. Explain what the people of Skara Brae made or used for these things.

Fire	
Clothing	
Mattress/Bed	
Insulation	
Fishing/Bait	

My learning log	While doing these activities:		
	I found Q _____ easy.	I found Q _____ challenging.	I found Q _____ interesting.

A Day at Skara Brae – 3

1. Find synonyms in the information above the diary for these words.

    (a) damaged _____   (b) violent _____

    (c) mixture _____   (d) made-up _____

2. Find antonyms in the diary entry for these words.

    (a) melting _____   (b) stale _____

    (c) dead _____   (d) released _____

3. Write the root word from which these words were made.

    (a) stripped _____   (b) imaginary _____

    (c) activities _____   (d) largest _____

    (e) extremely _____   (f) caused _____

    (g) completing _____   (h) nicer _____

4. In the word 'crochet', the 'ch' sounds like a 'sh'. Can you read the following words?

    | machine | chef | brochure | chalet | parachute | quiche |

5. Write the missing words in these sentences. Use question 4 to help you.

    (a) The _____ in the restaurant made a

       delicious ham and cheese _____.

    (b) Mum was looking through a holiday _____ for ideas.

    (c) The skydiver pulled the chord of his _____.

    (d) Dad was annoyed when his coffee _____ stopped working.

    (e) The _____ we stayed in was very modern and cosy.

My learning log	Colour:	I ⬚understand⬚ / ⬚need more practice on⬚ synonyms.
		I ⬚understand⬚ / ⬚need more practice on⬚ antonyms.
		I ⬚understand⬚ / ⬚need more practice on⬚ root words.

Life Cycle of a Mosquito

Read the explanation.

Did you know that a mosquito has a very short life cycle? Usually, it only lives between one week and one month.

A mosquito goes through four different stages during its life. These are the egg, larva, pupa and adult stages.

First, a female mosquito lays her eggs on the surface of some water. The water is still or very slow moving. It could be in a lake, a puddle in a ditch or even in a tree hole that holds water. She lays between 40 and 400 eggs in a raft shape.

An adult mosquito is forming inside each pupa. This takes a few days. Then each pupa's skin splits and an adult mosquito emerges. They dry their new wings before they fly off to look for food.

After a few days, larvae hatch out of the eggs. They stay just under the surface of the water. They breathe air through a tube. Larvae are sometimes called 'wrigglers' as they jerk their body to move. As larvae grow, they shed their skin and have a new one underneath.

Larvae shed their skin four times. This takes up to a week. Then they have become pupae. Pupae are sometimes called 'tumblers'. They also breathe air through tubes.

Another interesting fact about mosquitoes is what they eat. Male mosquitoes feed only on plant juices. However, most female mosquitoes need to drink animal blood. The blood makes their eggs healthy. So if you are bitten by a mosquito, you will know it's a female.

Life Cycle of a Mosquito

Assessment – Comprehension

1. The author has used a flow chart in the explanation.
   How does this help the reader to understand the life cycle?

   2 marks

   _____

2. Number these parts of the life cycle in the correct order.

   1 mark

   (a) The larva sheds its skin.

   (b) The larva becomes a pupa.

   (c) A female mosquito lays eggs.

   (d) The pupa's skin splits.

3. Mosquitoes' eggs are laid in still or slow-moving water.
   Why do you think this happens?

   2 marks

   _____

   _____

4. Tick one. A larva is different from a pupa because it:

   1 mark

   (a) breathes through a tube.   (b) lives in water.

   (c) sheds its skin four times.

5. Draw a line to match the names correctly.

   1 mark

   pupae •   • tumblers

   larvae •   • wrigglers

6. Name two things female mosquitoes do that males do not.

   1 mark

   _____

7. Tick the sentence that best explains what the text is mainly about.

   2 marks

   (a) A mosquito's life cycle is
        between one and four weeks.

   (b) A mosquito's life cycle includes
        larva and pupa.

   (c) A mosquito has four stages in its life cycle.

   | Total for this page | /10 |

Life Cycle of a Mosquito

Assessment – Word Reading

1. Find and write the plural form of these words.

1 mark

   (a) mosquito _____ (b) larva _____

   (c) pupa _____   (d) egg _____

2. What does the word 'emerges' mean in this sentence?
'Each pupa's skin splits and an adult mosquito emerges.'

1 mark

_____

_____

3. Find a word in the explanation that is a homophone for each word.
Write a sentence for each of the four words.

   (a) weak   _____

2 marks

   _____ _____

   (b) threw   _____

2 marks

   _____ _____

4. The words 'breathe' and 'breath' are confused words.
Write each in the correct sentence.

   (a) A mosquito larva can [_____] through a tube.

1 mark

   (b) For how long can you hold your [_____] ?

1 mark

5. The verb 'shed' in the sentence 'Larvae shed their skin four times'
means 'throw off'. The noun 'shed' means

1 mark

_____.

6. Larvae 'jerk' their body to move.
Which word could have been used instead? Tick one.

   (a) twitch [ ]   (b) glide [ ]   (c) leap [ ]

1 mark

Total for this page	/10	Total for this assessment	/20

Life Cycle of a Mosquito

Genre: Explanation

Breakdown of question type/content and mark allocation

Comprehension			Word Reading		
Q1.	Point of view and purpose	2 marks	Q1.	Plurals	1 mark
Q2.	Sequencing	1 mark	Q2.	Word meanings (context)	1 mark
Q3.	Inferring	2 marks	Q3.	Homophones (*weak/week; threw/through*)	4 marks
Q4.	Finding similarities and differences	1 mark	Q4.	Near-homophones (*breath/breathe*)	2 marks
Q5.	Understanding words	1 mark	Q5.	Word meaning differences (noun vs verb)	1 mark
Q6.	Concluding	1 mark	Q6.	Word meanings (synonyms)	1 mark
Q7.	Identifying the main idea	2 marks			
	Sub-total			Sub-total	
			Record the pupil's total result for this assessment.		

Assessment Answers

Assessment – Life Cycle of a Mosquito

Comprehension..*Page 79*

1. The flow chart has arrows which show the reader the correct order to follow in the life cycle./The flow chart continues in a circle like a life cycle.
2. (c), (a), (b), (d)
3. Answers should indicate that the eggs would split up and float away if the water moved swiftly.
4. (c)
5. pupae: tumblers, larvae: wrigglers
6. They lay eggs and drink blood.
7. (c)

Word Reading..*Page 80*

1. (a) mosquitoes (b) larvae (c) pupae (d) eggs
2. It means a mosquito comes out of a pupa.
3. (a) weak, week: Teacher check sentences.
   (b) threw, through: Teacher check sentences.
4. (a) breathe (b) breath
5. a hut or a cabin
6. (a)

The Legend of Tam O'Shanter

Curriculum Links

Activity	Code	Objective	Outcome
Text	C3 C6	• Listen to and discuss a wide range of fiction • Increase their familiarity with a wide range of books, including legends	• Can write an alternative ending for a legend
Comprehension	C5 C11 C13	• Use dictionaries to check the meaning of words that they have read • Check that the text makes sense to them, discuss their understanding and explain the meaning of words in context • Draw inferences such as inferring characters' feelings, thoughts and motives from their actions, and justifying inferences with evidence	• Can use a dictionary to find and check word meanings • Can retell a legend in their own words
Word Reading	WR1 WR2	• Apply their growing knowledge of root words and suffixes • Read further exception words, noting the unusual correspondences between spelling and sound	• Can use the suffix '-ly' to create new words • Can distinguish the spelling of different homophones

Additional Teacher Information

Definition of Terms

Narrative
A narrative is a text that tells a story. It includes a title, an orientation (setting, time and characters), a complication to the main character(s), a series of events, a resolution to the complication and an ending.

Legends
Legends are told as though the events were actual historical events. Legends may or may not be based on an elaborated version of a historical event. Legends are usually about human beings, although gods or fantasy beings such as witches may intervene in some way.

Collective nouns
Collective nouns are used to name groups of people, animals and things; e.g. crowd, flock, bunch.

Simile
A simile compares one thing to another. Similes make a description more emphatic or vivid. Similes are usually introduced by the words 'like' or 'as'.

Terminology for Pupils

legend
word
definition
phrase
collective noun
adjective
suffix
simile
homophone

Suggested Reading

• An online version and background information can be found at:

<http://myths.e2bn.org/mythsandlegends/story870-the-legend-of-tam-o-shanter.html>

• The original poem and translation can be found at:

<http://www.robertburns.org.uk/Assets/Poems_Songs/tamoshanter.htm>

Text

Teacher Information

- The imaginative text on page 85 is a narrative in the form of a legend. This legend was originally written as an epic 224-line narrative poem by the famous Scottish poet, Robert Burns in the late 1700s. It was set in his home village of Ayr (now a suburb of Alloway) in south-west Scotland and based on a local legend involving a fictional character Tam O' Shanter, who could have been an actual person, Douglas Graham of Shanter Farm in nearby Carrick. He was known to have a reputation for getting drunk on market days. It is interesting to note that 'cutty sark' was the name given to a famous clipper ship in the 1800s. This custom built clipper was built for bringing tea back from China. On her bough was the figurehead of the young witch in her cutty sark. In her outstretched left hand is a horse's tail.

Introduction

- Illustrations of the Cutty Sark ship could be shown to the pupils. Pupils could discuss how the ship looks compared to modern ships. Illustrations of the figurehead could also be viewed.

Development

- Read and discuss the legend with pupils, as a whole class or in groups. Assist pupils to decode new words if necessary. Discuss the meaning of any new or unfamiliar words and phrases. Question individual pupils to gauge their understanding of what they have listened to or read. Pupils should also ask questions about parts of the text they are unsure of, in order to improve their understanding of it.

- Tell the pupils to imagine that the young witch had managed to capture Tam O'Shanter. What might have happened next? Share ideas for alternative endings on the board.

Differentiated Individual/Paired/Group Work

- Pupils write an alternative ending to the legend, to tell what happened if the young witch had captured Tam O'Shanter.

- Less able pupils could write a few sentences and draw an illustration.

- More able pupils could write several paragraphs, in the style of the legend.

Review

- Pupils should share their work in a small group.

Comprehension

Teacher Information

- Pupils might need a dictionary to complete question 1.

Introduction

- Reread the legend. Ask pupils to focus on the sequence of events. Ask them to discuss the order of events in the legend.

Development

- Discuss possible answers to questions 7 and 8 as they may vary. Pupils need to justify a 'Yes' or 'No' answer to question 7.

- Remind pupils how to use a dictionary efficiently; i.e. alphabetical order and retrieval by 1st, 2nd and 3rd letters. Give each pupil, or pair of pupils, a dictionary. Write words from the text onto the board for pupils to find.

- Pupils take it in turns to retell the legend in their own words, sequencing the events correctly.

- Discuss the comprehension activities on page 86, then allow pupils to complete the page independently.

Differentiated Individual/Paired/Group Work

- Pupils summarise the legend using bullet points. Less able pupils could summarise the legend in six bullets points, whilst more able pupils could summarise in ten bullets points.

- More able pupils could read the original poem by Robert Burns. There is a translation available online at <http://www.robertburns.org.uk/Assets/Poems_Songs/tamoshanter.htm>.

Review

- As a class, compare pupils' answers to questions 7 and 8, as their answers will vary and will be interesting to compare. Do they think that Tam O'Shanter will go near the old ruined church again?

Word Reading

Teacher Information

- The activities on page 87 focus on collective nouns, adjectives, adverbs, the suffix '-ly', similes and homophones.

Introduction

- Reread the text, but first explain to the pupils that the focus will be on words. As they reread ask them to underline any homophones they see.

Development

- Explain the term 'collective noun' to the pupils as being a word for a group of specific items, animals or people; for example, a group of lions is called a pride. Give pupils a noun, and see if they know a collective noun for this item, animal or group of people. If this is too difficult, they could be prompted with a multiple-choice of answers. A quiz is available online at <http://www.vocabulary.cl/Games/collective-nouns.htm>.

- List other adjectives that could be used to describe Meg. What adjectives could be used to describe Tam and the young witch?

- Ensure pupils are familiar with the term 'homophone'. Give some examples (see/sea; there/their: maid/made). Elicit some examples from the pupils. Pupils suggest sentences for pairs of homophones, to be written onto the board; for example, son/sun = My parents have a son and a daughter./Planet Earth orbits around the sun.

- Discuss the word reading activities on page 87, then allow pupils to complete the page independently.

Differentiated Individual/Paired/Group Work

- Pupils should research and list collective nouns for groups of animals. Do some animals have more than one collective noun assigned to them?

- Less able pupils could be encouraged to find common collective nouns; for example, a pride of lions, a school of dolphins.

- More able pupils could be given less common collective nouns to search for, or asked to find animals that have more than one collective noun assigned to them.

Review

- As a class, compare pupils' lists of collective nouns. How many did they find? Did any of the collective nouns seem a little strange to them; for example, a murder of crows? Do any of the animals have two or more collective nouns?

Assessment

C3	Ask the pupils to write two alternative endings for the legend, one sad and one happy.
	Pupils should state which of their endings they prefer, and give reasons.
C5	Present the following list to the pupils and ask them to write them in alphabetical order:
	witch, warlock, wares, weather, window, women, wonderful
WR2	Write the following pairs of homophones on the board:
	meat/meet, piece/peace, plain/plane, great/grate, brake/break
	Ask the pupils to write each pair of words in a sentence.

Answers

Comprehension

1. (a) impressed (b) wares (c) muffled

2. Answers should indicate that he knew the church was meant to be haunted and visited by witches so went up carefully to avoid potential trouble.

3. unable to move because you are afraid

4. She was wearing a petticoat which is a 'cutty sark' in Scottish.

5. She had been galloping so hard that saliva was coming from her mouth.

6. (a), (d), (b), (c)

7. Pupils are more likely to say 'No' because he wouldn't have been able to reach the bridge as quickly by running himself compared with riding a galloping horse. 'Yes' answers could be accepted with justification; e.g. if the young witch could run fast, he could run faster.

8. Teacher check. Possible answers: Tam wouldn't go to the inn after market, he would go straight past the church and not look if he heard noises.

Word Reading

1. (a) crowds (b) coven

2. trusty, dependable, calm

3. regularly, particularly, cautiously, suddenly

4. (a) crumbling (b) dependable (c) cautiously
   (d) occasional (e) approached (f) particularly

5. swarmed, bees

6. (a) tail (b) knew (c) not (d) witch
   (e) led (f) heard (g) hear (h) weather
   (i) night (j) sell (k) made (l) where

The Legend of Tam O'Shanter – 1

Read this version of an old Scottish legend.

There once was a farmer named Tam O'Shanter who lived near the village of Alloway. Tam regularly visited Alloway to sell his wares at the busy marketplace.

After one particularly hectic day, where crowds of people swarmed like bees throughout the market, Tam decided to go to the local inn before he made his journey home. He left the inn quite late at night and mounted his trusty old mare, Meg. They set off down the road towards the moors. The weather had turned stormy and Tam could hear thunder in the distance. Occasional lightning flashes lit up the sky. As they approached an old, ruined church, Tam heard strange, chilling sounds coming from within the churchyard. The church was considered to be haunted and a place where witches gathered.

Cautiously, Tam led Meg closer to the church to find out what was happening. Peering through a crumbling window arch he let out a muffled gasp. There in the middle of the churchyard was a huge bonfire. A coven of witches and warlocks were dancing and singing around the flames.

Tam sat rigid with fear on his calm, dependable mare. He gazed open-mouthed at the group of ugly old women and men. He noticed, however, that one of the witches was not an old hag but young and beautiful. She was wearing a short petticoat called a 'cutty sark' in the old Scottish language. Tam was so impressed with her wonderful dancing that he forgot his fear and called out: 'Well done Cutty Sark!'

Suddenly, the bonfire went out and a terrible howl came from the witches and warlocks. They began racing full speed towards Tam, intent on catching this man who had interrupted their private gathering. Meg had already started to gallop away and Tam spurred her on even faster. Together they raced towards the nearby bridge over the River Doon. Tam knew that witches could not cross over running water.

With Meg foaming at the mouth they neared the bridge. But the young witch had almost caught up with them. Just as they reached the bridge, she made one final lunge and caught Meg's tail. Meg made a desperate leap forward with Tam clinging to her back. A large clump of Meg's tail was all the witch found in her hand. Tam was safe! He patted Meg and thanked her for his narrow escape.

My learning log	When I read this legend, I could read:	☐ all of it. ☐ most of it. ☐ parts of it.

The Legend of Tam O'Shanter – 2

1. Match each word with its correct definition.

   (a) filled with admiration •   • muffled

   (b) articles for sale   •   • impressed

   (c) deadened the sound to make it quieter •   • wares

2. Why did Tam lead Meg cautiously towards the churchyard?

   _____

3. What does the phrase 'rigid with fear' mean?

   _____

4. Why did Tam call the young witch 'Cutty Sark'?

   _____

5. Why was Meg 'foaming at the mouth'? _____

   _____

6. Order these events from 1 to 4.

   (a) Tam peeked through a crumbling window arch. ☐

   (b) The young witch grabbed at Meg's tail. ☐

   (c) Meg made a desperate leap forward. ☐

   (d) The witches and warlocks raced towards Tam. ☐

7. (a) Do you think Tam would have reached
        the safety of the bridge on his own?   ⌐ Yes ⌐ ⌐ No ⌐

   (b) Explain your answer. _____

   _____

8. What do you think Tam O'Shanter might learn from his narrow escape?

   _____

   _____

My learning log	While doing these activities:		
	I found Q _____ easy.	I found Q _____ challenging.	I found Q _____ interesting.

The Legend of Tam O'Shanter – 3

1. A collective noun is used to name groups of things; e.g. a class of children. Which collective noun is used in the text for these groups?

   (a) _____ of people at the market

   (b) _____ of witches and warlocks

2. Write three adjectives from the legend that describe Meg's character.

   _____   _____   _____

3. The suffix '-ly' is added to an adjective to form an adverb. Find four adverbs in the text with this suffix.

   _____   _____   _____   _____

4. Add one of these suffixes to each root word to make words in the text. (Check the spelling in the text!)

-ly	-al	-able	-ed	-ing

   (a) crumble _____   (b) depend _____

   (c) cautious _____   (d) occasion _____

   (e) approach _____   (f) particular _____

5. A simile compares one thing to another; e.g. sharp like a knife. What did the writer compare the crowds of people in the market to?

   crowds of people _____ like _____

6. Which word from the text is a homophone for each word below?

   (a) tale _____   (b) new _____

   (c) knot _____   (d) which _____

   (e) lead _____   (f) herd _____

   (g) here _____   (h) whether _____

   (i) knight _____   (j) cell _____

   (k) maid _____   (l) ware _____

My learning log	*Colour:*	I ⎡can recognise⎤ / ⎡am not too sure about⎤ collective nouns.
		I ⎡know⎤ / ⎡don't know⎤ how to use the suffix '-ly'.
		I ⎡understand⎤ / ⎡need more practice on⎤ homophones.

What's Going to Happen to Us?

Curriculum Links

Activity	Code	Objective	Outcome
Text	C3 C4 C6	• Listen to and discuss a wide range of plays • Read books that are structured in different ways • Increase their familiarity with a wide range of books	• Can identify key features of a play
Comprehension	C11 C13 C16	• Check that the text makes sense to them, discuss their understanding and explain the meaning of words in context • Draw inferences such as inferring characters' feelings, thoughts and motives from their actions, and justifying inferences with evidence • Identify how language, structure and presentation contribute to meaning	• Can explain the meanings of words • Can identify characters' feelings • Can identify features of a play
Word Reading	WR1 WR2	• Apply their growing knowledge of root words and prefixes • Read further exception words, noting the unusual correspondences between spelling and sound	• Can use the prefixes 're-', 'un-', 'dis-' and 'mis-' to create new words • Can distinguish the spelling of different homophones

Additional Teacher Information

Definition of Terms

Playscripts

Plays are specific pieces of drama, usually performed on a stage, with a number of actors in make-up and wearing appropriate costumes.

Links to other Curriculum Areas

• PSHE – Importance of recycling

Terminology for Pupils

playscript
scene/setting
character
conversation
fiction
non-fiction
prefix
root word
definition
homophone

Suggested Reading

• *Recycle* by Gail Gibbons
• *World-wide Waste* by Caren Trafford

Text

Teacher Information

- The play on page 91 includes fictional characters in the form of inanimate objects that are able to speak. These characters give facts about recycling and reusing, so the text is a combination of fiction and non-fiction.

Introduction

- Discuss the features of the play; the setting described in the 'Scene', and the characters' names in bold to the left of what each one says.

Development

- Due to space restrictions, this play does not have detailed stage directions. Pupils could add some stage directions; for example, the first line Box recites could have a direction to look sad and put his/her arm around Tray. When written in a play, these directions are put in brackets in italic script.

- Ask pupils what household items their family recycles. What do they do with cardboard, cans, plastic packaging, newspapers and glass to recycle them? Do they recycle clothes or shoes? Where can these be recycled? What happens to garden waste? Are there any items from their home that do not get recycled?

- Read and discuss the play with the pupils. Assist pupils to decode new words if necessary. Question individual pupils to gauge their understanding of what they have listened to or read. Pupils should also ask questions about parts of the play they are unsure of, in order to improve their understanding of it.

Differentiated Individual/Paired/Group Work

- Working in mixed ability groups of four, pupils could add some stage directions before reading the play, adding appropriate intonation, tone, volume and action.

- Each group should prepare a performance of the play. Less able pupils could play the parts of Box or Tray, as these characters have less to read.

Review

- Groups should perform their plays to the class.

Comprehension

Teacher Information

- Pupils will need to understand the difference between recycling and reusing.

Introduction

- Discuss the features of a play; for example, setting, list of characters and stage directions. Another play should be looked at, which has these features.

Development

- Pupils describe what is going to happen to each character in the play. Will they be recycled or reused?

- Discuss the meaning of fiction and non-fiction. Why could this play be described as being a mixture of both?

- Discuss the comprehension activities on page 92, then allow pupils to complete the page independently.

Differentiated Individual/Paired/Group Work

- Pupils suggest how the following items could be recycled *and* reused: cereal box, newspaper, empty food can, plastic bottle, plastic cake tray, glass jar. For example, a glass jar could be recycled in a recycling centre by being made into another glass object or could be reused as a pot to put pencils in.

- More able pupils could use the Internet to find out what happens to the different items that are collected for recycling. What are the items made into?

Review

- As a class, discuss ways of reusing household items. Which ideas are the most imaginative?

Word Reading

Teacher Information

- The activities on page 93 focus on the prefixes 're-', 'un-', 'dis-' and 'mis-', root words and homophones.
- Pupils will need a dictionary to complete question 1(c).

Introduction

- Reread the text, but first explain to pupils that the focus will be on words. As they reread, ask them to underline any homophones they see.

Development

- Explain that the prefix 're-' means 'again' or 'back'. How do the words 'recycle' and 'reuse' have these meanings? Can the pupils think of any other words with this prefix? How do they mean 'again' or 'back'?
- Ensure pupils are familiar with the term 'homophone'. Give some examples (see/sea; there/their; maid/made). Elicit some examples from the pupils. Pupils suggest sentences for pairs of homophones, to be written onto the board; for example, son/sun = My parents have a <u>son</u> and a daughter./Planet Earth orbits around the <u>sun</u>.
- Look at words with the prefix 'un-'. Discuss how adding this prefix makes the words negative; for example, 'do' becomes 'undo' and 'expected' becomes 'unexpected'. Write sentences containing the pairs of words; for example, Peter was *kind* to Marissa, but *unkind* to me.
- Discuss the word reading activities on page 93, then allow pupils to complete the page independently.

Differentiated Individual/Paired/Group Work

- Pupils should research the prefixes that give words a negative meaning; i.e. 'un-', 'dis-' and 'mis-'. They should use a dictionary to write a list of words with each prefix.

un-	dis-	mis-
unkind	disable	misbehave
unwell	disappoint	mislead
unhappy	disagree	misspell
unable	disobey	

- Less able pupils could write sentences for some of the words.
- More able pupils could write a paragraph using as many of these negative words as possible.

Review

- As a class, compare pupils' lists of negative words. Which prefix is the most and least common?

Assessment

C3	Ask the pupils to choose one of the characters. They should write a short play, using this character and new characters, that tells what happens when the character arrives to be recycled or reused; for example, the Box at the paper recycling centre, the Can at the can recycling centre, the Tray at the school, and the Boots at the charity shop.
C11	Present the following word list to the pupils and ask them to write a definition for each: recycle, reuse, charity, germs, rubbish, decompose
WR1	Call out (or write on the board) the following words and have pupils place them in four different grids, according to the prefixes that can be added to them ('re-', 'un-', 'dis-', 'mis-'): decorate, manage, advantage, comfortable, please, fortune, fill, hook, fuel, agree, fire, afraid

Answers

Comprehension

1. To teach the reader about recycling and reusing.
2. In a kitchen on a table.
3. (a) Can (b) Boots (c) Box (d) Tray
4. (a) They were unhappy and thought something bad was going to happen to them.
   (b) They were pleased because they realised they would be recycled or reused.
5. (a) fiction and non-fiction
   (b) Answers should indicate that the information about recycling and reusing is true but objects like cans, boots, boxes and trays can't speak.
6. (a) Can and Box will both be recycled.
   (b) Boots will be reused by being sold and worn again and Tray will be reused by being taken to school for another purpose.
7. Teacher check

Word Reading

1. (a) recycled, recycling, reused
   (b) It means 'again' or 'back'.
   (c) Teacher check
2. (a) Recycling is turning used things into new things that can be used again. Reusing is using the same thing again in a different way.
   (b) Teacher check
3. (a) landfill   (b) buried   (c) separated
   (d) worried   (e) exciting   (f) decompose(s)
4. (a) low in price (b) Teacher check
5. un
6. (a) un   (b) dis   (c) mis
   (d) mis   (e) un   (f) dis
   (g) dis   (h) mis   (i) un

Read the play.

Scene: *An empty soft drink can, a pizza box, a polystyrene meat tray and a pair of boots are sitting on the kitchen table. Can and Boots are smiling, while Box and Tray look most unhappy.*

Box: Why are you looking so happy Can and Boots? Tray and I have an awful feeling something bad is going to happen to us.

Can: Well I'm going to be recycled. That's not bad. It's great!

Tray: What's recycling? What'll happen to you?

Can: Recycling is turning used things into new things that can be used again. I'll be collected by a lorry and taken to a recycling centre and made into another soft drink can.

Boots: I'm happy because I'm going to be reused. Oscar's feet have grown so much that he can't fit into me anymore. But I look almost new. I'm going to a charity shop where someone will buy me for a cheap price. I'll have new owners. How exciting!

Tray: I'm worried. I can't be recycled because I'm made of a type of foam. Can I be reused like you, Boots?

Boots: You'll be reused. Oscar's teacher gets his class to collect trays like you. The class uses them to put blobs of paint on during art lessons. Then you'll be washed and stored for another time.

Box: Can or Boots ... can I be reused or recycled?

Can: Cardboard boxes can be reused if they are clean. You can't be reused because you have pizza bits stuck to your insides and germs can grow there. But you can be recycled. Cardboard is made into different kinds of paper products.

Tray: What happens to things that can't be recycled or reused?

Boots: They get buried in enormous holes in the ground called landfill sites. Some of the rubbish decomposes and adds nutrients to the soil. Other rubbish will not decompose and will still be in the soil for hundreds of years.

Box: So people must recycle and reuse as much as possible so the world doesn't become a huge rubbish tip!

Can: That's right, Box. Look! Here comes Oscar's mum. It's time for us to be separated. Nice chatting with you all!

My learning log	When I read this play, I could read:	☐ all of it. ☐ most of it. ☐ parts of it.

What's Going to Happen to Us? – 2

1. What is the purpose of the play?

   _____

2. Where is the setting of the play? _____

3. Which character:

   (a) explains what recycling is?

   (b) explains what reusing is?

   (c) can't be reused for health reasons?

   (d) is made from a non-recyclable product?

4. (a) How did Box and Tray feel at the beginning of the conversation?

      _____

   (b) Describe how they felt at the end.

      _____

5. (a) Is this play fiction, non-fiction or a mixture of both? _____

   (b) Explain your answer. _____

      _____

6. With regard to what will happen in the future, how are:

   (a) Can and Box similar? _____

   (b) Boots and Tray different? _____

      _____

      _____

7. Describe a way each thing could be recycled or reused.

   (a) honey jar _____

   (b) plastic takeaway container _____

My learning log	While doing these activities:		
	I found Q _____ easy.	I found Q _____ challenging.	I found Q _____ interesting.

1. (a)   Find three words in the text with the prefix 're-'.

_____   _____   _____

(b)   What meaning does this prefix add? _____

(c)   Use a dictionary to find four other words with this prefix.

_____   _____   _____   _____

2. (a)   What is the difference between recycling and reusing?

_____

_____

(b)   Name something that your family have recycled and reused.

recycled: _____   reused: _____

3. Write the word from the play made from each root word.

(a)   land   _____   (b)   bury   _____

(c)   separate   _____   (d)   worry   _____

(e)   excite   _____   (f)   compose   _____

4. (a)   In the play, what does the word 'cheap' mean? _____

(b)   Give a definition for its homophone 'cheep'. _____

5. Can and Boots are happy, but Box and Tray are unhappy.

Which prefix makes the 'happy' feeling negative? _____

6. The prefixes 'un-', 'dis-' and 'mis-' all give words negative meanings. Add one of these prefixes to the following words to make them negative.

(a)   ___happy   (b)   ___appoint   (c)   ___lead

(d)   ___behave   (e)   ___kind   (f)   ___agree

(g)   ___obey   (h)   ___take   (i)   ___cover

My learning log	*Colour:*	I know / don't know about the prefix 're-'.
		I can recognise / am not too sure about root words.
		I understand / need more practice adding prefixes to make words negative.

Curriculum Links

Activity	Code	Objective	Outcome
Text	C3 C6	• Listen to and discuss a wide range of non-fiction and reference books • Increase their familiarity with a wide range of books	• Can identify key features of a non-fiction text organised by steps
Comprehension	C11 C15	• Check that the text makes sense to them, discuss their understanding and explain the meaning of words in context • Identify main ideas from more than one paragraph and summarise these	• Can use a dictionary to find and check word meanings • Can summarise/give the main idea of a paragraph
Word Reading	WR1 WR2	• Apply their growing knowledge of root words and suffixes • Read further exception words, noting the unusual correspondences between spelling and sound	• Can use a range of suffixes • Can recognise the /s/ sound spelt 'sc' • Can distinguish the spelling of different homophones

Additional Teacher Information

Definition of Terms

Report
Reports are written documents describing the findings of an individual or group about a specific subject.

Procedure
A procedure is a text that outlines how something is made or done. Its purpose is to inform the reader. A procedure may be written in the form of a recipe, instructions for making something, an experiment, how to play a game, how to use an appliance and so on. A procedure usually includes numbered concise instructions beginning with imperative verbs.

Fact
Something that is true or real.

Opinion
A view or judgement formed about something, not necessarily based on fact or knowledge.

Links to other Curriculum Areas

• History – Achievement of early civilisations; i.e. the Ancient Egyptian mummification process

Terminology for Pupils

procedure
non-fiction
definition
fact/opinion
paragraph
antonym
synonym
suffix
root word
homophone

Suggested Reading

• This website includes lots of facts about Ancient Egypt and mummies suitable for this age group:

 <http://primaryhomeworkhelp.co.uk/ egypt/mummies.htm>

• *Everything Ancient Egypt* by **Crispin Boyer** (National Geographic series)

• *Mummies Made in Egypt* by **Aliki**

• *Mummies in the Morning* by **Mary Pope Osborne**

Text

Teacher Information

- The informative text on Ancient Egyptian mummies on page 97 has a short introduction with facts about the process of mummification and why it was followed. A procedure outlining the main steps completes the report. This procedure is not the same as those that use an imperative verb to begin each new instruction as it is more of an explanation.

Introduction

- Ask pupils if any of them have ever been to a museum. What kind of artefacts were on display? Were there any artefacts from Ancient Egypt? Were there mummies or canopic jars?

- Provide colour images of mummies and the process of mummification from non-fiction books or from the *Suggested Reading* list on the previous page for pupils to view.

Development

- Discuss how steps in a procedure help the reader to understand how to complete a process. Talk about other texts that are organized by steps; for example, art and craft books, recipes.

- Read and discuss the procedure with the pupils. Assist pupils to decode new words if necessary. Question individual pupils to gauge their understanding of what they have listened to or read. Pupils should also ask questions about parts of the text they are unsure of, in order to improve their understanding of it.

Differentiated Individual/Paired/Group Work

- Pupils write a procedure explaining how to make something; for example, a sock puppet.

- Less able pupils could write a procedure using six steps.

- More able pupils could write a procedure using at least ten steps.

Review

- Pupils should share their work in a small group.

Comprehension

Teacher Information

- Pupils may need a dictionary to complete question 1.

Introduction

- Pupils take it in turns to summarise each step in their own words.

Development

- Remind pupils how to use a dictionary efficiently; i.e. alphabetical order and retrieval by 1st, 2nd and 3rd letters. Give each pupil, or pair of pupils, a dictionary. Write words from the text onto the board for pupils to find.

- Discuss the comprehension activities on page 98, then allow pupils to complete the page independently.

Differentiated Individual/Paired/Group Work

- Pupils create a glossary for some of the more technical vocabulary in the procedure; for example, preserve, mummy, purify, ritual, lungs, intestines, liver, heart, brain, natron, canopic jars, ointment, sawdust, linen.

- Less able pupils could create a glossary for six words, more able pupils for all fourteen words.

Review

- As a class, compare pupils' definitions of the words. Which words were the hardest and easiest to define?

Word Reading

Teacher Information

- The activities on page 99 focus on the /s/ sound spelt 'sc', synonyms, antonyms, a range of suffixes, root words, homophones and origins of words.

Introduction

- Reread the text, but first explain to pupils that the focus will be on words. As they reread, ask them to underline any homophones they see.

Development

- Ensure pupils are familiar with the terms 'synonym' and 'antonym'. Give some examples (happy: synonym is glad, antonym is sad). Elicit some examples from the pupils. Pupils suggest sentences for pairs of synonyms and antonyms, to be written onto the board; for example, happy = *glad/sad*. Ben was glad he had homework, but Krista was sad.

- Look at words with the suffix '-ation'. Discuss how the suffix is added straight onto the end of the root word; for example, information. But if the root word ends in 'e', the 'e' is first dropped; for example, adoration, sensation. Note that words of more than one syllable, ending in a vowel and then 'l', double the final 'l' before adding the suffix; for example, cancellation.

- Ensure pupils are familiar with the term 'homophone'. Give some examples (see/sea; there/their; maid/made). Elicit some examples from the pupils. Pupils suggest sentences for pairs of homophones, to be written onto the board; for example, son/sun = My parents have a son and a daughter./Planet Earth orbits around the sun.

- Discuss the word reading activities on page 99, then allow pupils to complete the page independently.

Differentiated Individual/Paired/Group Work

- Give pupils pairs of homophones to match; for example, meat/meet, brake/break. In groups, pupils could simply match the cards or play a version of 'Snap'.

- Once the cards have been sorted, pupils could write sentences using the homophones. Less able pupils could write a separate sentence for each word in the pair, whilst more able pupils could write one sentence containing both homophones; for example, Mum said to *meet* her in the *meat* aisle of the supermarket.

Review

- In a group, pupils read and compare their sentences.

Assessment

C15	Ask the pupils to write a summary of the ten steps, combining them to make only six or eight steps. Remind them that the steps need to be kept in the correct order.
C11	Present the following list of words to the pupils and ask them to write a definition for each: preserve, complicated, ceremony, hook, discard, ointment
WR2	Call out (or write on the board) the following words and have pupils place them in two different grids, according to the shared 'sc' sound: science, scary, scene, scatter, scent, scorpion, discipline, school, fascinate, crescent, scale, scanner

Answers

Comprehension

1. (a) to make clean and pure
   (b) kept from going bad
   (c) a soft, greasy substance used on skin
   (d) threw away
   (e) salt
2. (a) opinion (b) fact (c) fact
3. It explains why the Ancient Egyptians made mummies.
4. (a) heart
   (b) It was believed the heart did all the thinking.
5. (a) It dried out the organs, and inside and outside of body.
   (b) Put in body to help keep its shape.
   (c) Wrapped around body to keep everything in place.
6. dried out with natron, wrapped and placed in special jars, buried with the mummy

Word Reading

1. (a) fascinating
   (b) science, scene, discipline, scissors, crescent
2. (a) most (b) preserved (c) death
   (d) complicated
3. (a) internal (b) removed (c) small
   (d) placed (e) stuffed (f) packets
4. (a) wrapped (b) fascinating (c) mummification
   (d) lengthy (e) carefully (f) purified
5. (a) through (b) Teacher check
6. before

Mummy Makers – 1

Read the information text.

One of the most fascinating things to learn about the Ancient Egyptians is how they preserved a body after death and made it into a mummy. This process is called mummification. It was a very complicated and lengthy procedure to follow and took up to 70 days to complete.

Why did the Ancient Egyptians want to make mummies? They believed that when they died they would travel to another world and lead a new life. For this to happen, they needed to preserve their body. The main steps were:

1. The dead body was washed and purified by performing special rituals or ceremonies.

2. Internal organs like the lungs, intestines and liver were carefully removed through a small hole made in the left side. Only the heart was left as it was believed the heart did all the thinking.

3. These organs were covered in a mineral salt called 'natron' to dry them out. Later, they were wrapped and placed in special jars.

4. Using a hook, the brain was pulled out in pieces through the nostrils. It was discarded.

5. The inside of the body was stuffed with small packets of natron.

6. The outside of the body was covered in natron and left to dry out.

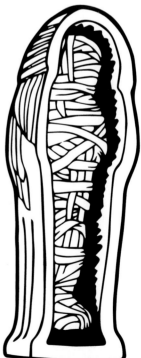

7. The body was cleaned to remove the natron. It was then rubbed with ointment to preserve the skin and head.

8. The packets of natron were taken out of the body and replaced with sawdust and linen so the body would keep its shape.

9. The small hole in the left side was sewn up.

10. The body was wrapped in layers of linen strips to keep everything in place. The mummy was now ready for burial along with the organs in the jars.

| My learning log | When I read this procedure, I could read: | ☐ all of it. | ☐ most of it. | ☐ parts of it. |

Mummy Makers – 2

1. Match each word to its definition.

   (a) purified •   • a soft, greasy substance used on skin

   (b) preserved •   • threw away

   (c) ointment •   • to make clean and pure

   (d) discarded •   • kept from going bad

   (e) natron •   • salt

2. Fact or opinion?

   (a) Mummies are fascinating things to learn about.   [Fact] [Opinion]

   (b) The brain was removed through the nostrils.   [Fact] [Opinion]

   (c) Mummification took more than two months
       to complete.   [Fact] [Opinion]

3. What is the main idea of paragraph 2? _____

   _____

4. (a) Which organ was not taken out of the body? _____

   (b) Why was this not removed like the others? _____

   _____

5. Explain why these things were used.

   (a) natron _____

   (b) sawdust and linen _____

   (c) linen strips _____

6. What three things happened to the organs taken from the body through the
   left side?

   • _____

   • _____

   • _____

My learning log	While doing these activities:		
	I found Q _____ easy.	I found Q _____ challenging.	I found Q _____ interesting.

Mummy Makers – 3

1. (a) Find a word in the text that has the /s/ sound spelt 'sc'. _____

   (b) Circle the following words that also have this sound.

   | science | school | scene | scarecrow |
   | discipline | scissors | scandal | crescent |

2. Find antonyms in the first paragraph for these words.

   (a) least _____   (b) destroyed _____

   (c) life _____   (d) easy _____

3. Find synonyms in the steps for these words. The number of the step where you will find the answer is in brackets.

   (a) inner (2) _____   (b) extracted (2) _____

   (c) little (2) _____   (d) put (3) _____

   (e) filled (5) _____   (f) packages (8) _____

4. Add one of the these suffixes to each root word to make words in the text. (Check the spelling in the text.)

   | -y | -ing | -ed | -fully | -ation |

   (a) wrap _____   (b) fascinate _____

   (c) mummify _____   (d) length _____

   (e) care _____   (f) purify _____

5. (a) The words 'through' and 'threw' are homophones. Use the correct word to complete this sentence from the text.

   The internal organs were removed _____ a small hole.

   (b) Write a sentence using the other homophone.

   _____

6. The word 'ancient' comes from a Latin word 'ante' which means '_____'.

My learning log	*Colour:*	I ⌐can recognise⌐ / ⌐am not too sure about⌐ the /s/ sound spelt 'sc'.
		I ⌐understand⌐ / ⌐need more practice on⌐ synonyms and antonyms.
		I ⌐know⌐ / ⌐don't know⌐ when to add different suffixes to root words.

Mummy has the Last Laugh

Curriculum Links

Activity	Code	Objective	Outcome
Text	C3	• Listen to and discuss a wide range of fiction	• Can identify key features of a newspaper report
Comprehension	C5 C11 C16	• Use dictionaries to check the meaning of words that they have read • Check that the text make sense to them, discuss their understanding and explain the meaning of words in context • Identify how language contributes to meaning	• Can use a dictionary to find and check word meanings • Can retell a recount in their own words
Word Reading	WR1 WR2	• Apply their growing knowledge of root words and prefixes • Read further exception words, noting the unusual correspondences between spelling and sound	• Can use the prefix 'un-' to create new words • Can recognise the '/k/' sound spelt 'ch' and the /ı/ sound spelt 'y' • Can distinguish the spelling of different homophones

Additional Teacher Information

Definition of Terms

Recount

A recount is a text which retells events as they happened in time order. It can be imaginative, factual or personal. A recount can be written in the form of a newspaper report, a diary, email, letter, journal, conversation, interview, biography, autobiography or eyewitness account. Its purpose is to inform or entertain, or both.

Newspaper report/article

Most reporters follow an 'inverted pyramid' style of writing news articles.

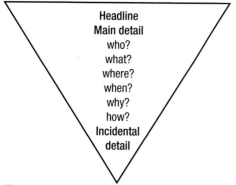

Headline
Main detail
who?
what?
where?
when?
why?
how?
Incidental
detail

Headline

A headline gives an overview of an article's content. It is usually short in length, attention-grabbing and sets the tone of the article (serious, shocking, humorous etc.)

Lead sentence

Similar to a headline but entices the reader to continue.

Links to other Curriculum Areas

• History – Achievements of early civilisations; i.e. the Ancient Egyptian mummies

Terminology for Pupils

newspaper report
newspaper article
caption
photograph
headline
homophone
prefix
paragraph

Suggested Reading

• The following website includes lots of facts about Ancient Egypt and mummies suitable for this age group:

<http://primaryhomeworkhelp.co.uk/egypt/mummies.htm>

• *Everything Ancient Egypt* by Crispin Boyer (National Geographic series)

• *Mummies made in Egypt* by Aliki

• *Mummies in the Morning* by Mary Pope Osborne

Text

Teacher Information

- The text on page 103 is an imaginative recount in the form of a newspaper article. While fictitious, it does include some technical language relating to facts about Ancient Egypt.

Introduction

- Ask pupils if any of them have ever been to a museum. Have a class discussion on the kind of museums open to the public (history, art, science). What kind of artefacts were on display? Were there any artefacts from Ancient Egypt?

Development

- Write the following words onto the board: *Ancient Egypt*, *mummy*, *museum*, *curator*, *fake*, *sarcophagus*, *exhibition*, *artefacts*, *coffin*. Discuss the meaning of these words. Show pupils photographs of a mummy and sarcophagus.

- Explore the British Museum's children's website to enhance children's understanding: <www.ancientegypt.co.uk>

   The British Museum's Children's online tours include a section 'Journey into the Mummy' at <www.britishmuseum.org. explore/young>

- Ask pupils if they know what special name is given to 1st April. What do some people do on this day? Have the pupils ever played a trick on someone on April Fool's Day? What happened? Has anyone ever played an April Fool's Day trick on them? What happened?

- Read and discuss the article with the pupils. Assist pupils to decode new words if necessary. Question individual pupils to gauge their understanding of what they have listened to or read. Pupils should also ask questions about parts of the text they're unsure of, in order to improve their understanding of it.

Differentiated Individual/Paired/Group Work

- Tell the pupils to imagine that the children at the museum didn't realise the mummy was an actor in costume. They thought it was a real mummy. What might have happened next? Have groups come up with ideas for alternative endings on the board.

- Pupils write an alternative ending to the newspaper article, to replace the final three paragraphs.

- Less able pupils could write a few sentences and draw an illustration.

- More able pupils could continue writing in the style of the newspaper article, including interviews with the schoolchildren, teachers, tour guide and actor.

Review

- Pupils should share their work in a small group.

Comprehension

Teacher Information

- Pupils will need a dictionary to complete question 1.

Introduction

- Discuss the title with the class. Ask if the title gives any clues to the content of the text. Reread the text, asking pupils to underline any vocabulary they need to explore.

Development

- Assist pupils to identify features of a newspaper report; e.g. headline, lead sentence, captions accompanying photographs and other visuals, details (who, what, when, why, how), quoted speech from interviews conducted by the reporter.

- Remind pupils how to use a dictionary efficiently; i.e. alphabetical order. Practise this skill. Give each pupil, or pair of pupils, a dictionary and ask them to find words such as museum/music/muscle. Teach that when words begin with the same letter each subsequent letter is treated in alphabetical order. Write words from the text onto the board for pupils to find.

- Pupils take it in turns to retell part of the recount in their own words, sequencing the events correctly.

- Discuss the comprehension activities on page 104, then allow pupils to complete the page independently.

Differentiated Individual/Paired/Group Work

- Pupils summarise the newspaper article using bullet points.

- Less able pupils could summarise the article in six bullet points, whilst more able pupils could summarise in ten bullet points.

Review

- As a class, compare pupils' answers to question 7 as their answers will vary and will be interesting to compare. Which is their favourite headline and why?

Word Reading

Teacher Information

- The activities on page 105 focus on homophones, etymology, the prefix 'un-', root words and the sounds 'y' and 'ch'.

Introduction

- Explain to the pupils that today they will reread the text, this time focusing on features of words. As they reread, ask them to underline any homophones they see.

Development

- Ensure pupils are familiar with the term 'homophone'. Give some examples (see/sea; there/their; maid/made). Elicit some examples from the pupils. Pupils suggest sentences for pairs of homophones, to be written onto the board; for example, son/sun = My parents have a <u>son</u> and a daughter./Planet Earth orbits around the <u>sun</u>.

- Discuss question 3, as this contains difficult vocabulary and needs some knowledge of etymology.

- Look at words with the prefix 'un-'. Discuss how adding this prefix makes the words negative; for example, 'do' becomes 'undo' and 'expected' becomes 'unexpected'. Write sentences containing the pairs of words; for example, Peter was <u>kind</u> to Marissa, but <u>unkind</u> to me.

- The 'y' and 'ch' words in questions 5 and 6 should be spoken out loud, so pupils can hear the specific phonemes focused upon.

- Discuss the word reading activities on page 105, then allow pupils to complete the page independently.

Differentiated Individual/Paired/Group Work

- In pairs, pupils should find and list words with a 'ch' spelling; for example, 'school', 'scheme', 'character', 'chemist', 'chip', 'children', 'cheek'. Then they should sort them according to their 'ch' sound.

- Less able pupils could sort the two types of 'ch' sounds covered on page 105, whilst more able pupils could sort three types of 'ch' sound, introducing the 'ch' sound of French origin; for example, 'chalet', 'chef'.

'ch' as in 'children'	'ch' as in 'school' (Greek origin)	'ch' as in 'chef' (French origin)
children, approached, charger, chicken	character, chemist, echo, chorus	chalet, machine, brochure, chef

Review

- As a class, compare pupils' lists of 'ch' words. Which of the sounds has the greatest number of words?

Assessment

C16	Ask the pupils to write words they have learned by giving them the meaning and not the actual word. For example, say: Write the word that means: a stone coffin; to appear/to come out of; the head of a museum or gallery. Where pupils are finding difficulty in writing the words, they can refer to the activity sheet. Note as part of the assessment, those pupils that could identify and spell the words independently and those that required help.
C5	Present the following list of words to the pupils and ask them to write them in alphabetical order: metropolis, mechanic, mascot, measure, message, metric, microphone
WR2	Call out (or write on the board) the following words and have pupils place them in two different grids, according to the shared sound: chemistry, cheap, choose, echo, anchor, itch, monarch, stomach, chop, lunch, champ, architect

Answers

Comprehension

1. (a) aiming to create an effect
   (b) a stone coffin
   (c) gave news or knowledge to
   (d) came out into sight
   (e) a person who looks after a museum
   (f) objects made by humans, often in the distant past

2. Answers should indicate that the museum curator thought visitors would enjoy seeing a fake mummy, as Ancient Egypt was a popular theme.

3. Answers should indicate that the tour group was not informed about the mummy like the others. The children were frightened instead of being pleased.

4. April Fool's Day is on 1 April. The date of the newspaper is 2 April and the article mentions 'yesterday'.

5. tour guide, child

6. (a) A stunt comes undone (b) The wording means the stunt didn't go as planned and it also matches the undone bandages.

7. Teacher check

Word Reading

1. (a) due   (b) to   (c) their
   (d) been   (e) not   (f) would

2. (a) bee   (b) site   (c) sew   (d) reel

3. Answers should indicate there is a body inside a coffin and after time the flesh is eaten away by decay.

4. (a) <u>un</u>do, <u>un</u>expected
   (b) It gives each word an opposite meaning.

5. (a) myth, gym, pyramid, mystery
   (b) towards the front of the word, and not last

6. schoolchildren, Teacher check

Read the newspaper article.

NATIONAL TIMES

2 April

Mummy has the Last Laugh

A stunt comes undone

A theatrical stunt at the National Museum yesterday did not go as planned when a class of schoolchildren thought they were being attacked by a 4000-year-old mummy.

Due to the increasing popularity of films about Ancient Egypt, the museum curator decided to give visitors a treat. He hired an actor to dress up as a mummy and come out of a fake sarcophagus during group tours of their Ancient Egyptian exhibition.

All tour guides had been told to inform their groups about the stunt before entering the area displaying Ancient Egyptian artefacts. Until yesterday, visitors were delighted with the mummy's performance.

The tour guide in charge of this particular school group's tour decided not to mention the mummy.

'It was April Fool's Day and I thought it would be fun to play a trick on the children', the tour guide explained, when asked why the group was not informed.

As the children approached the sarcophagus for a closer look, the actor, dressed as mummy, emerged from the coffin.

The children began screaming in terror at this completely unexpected sight.

Meanwhile, the actor tripped over his bandages trying to undo them to show he was not actually a mummy.

'It was so scary', one child said. 'We thought it was real. It was worse when he started taking off the bandages because we didn't know what would be underneath.'

The mummy stunt eventually ended in laughter when the children realised the half-wrapped person lying on the floor with a big grin on his face was definitely not a mummy.

| **My learning log** | When I read this newspaper article, I could read: ☐ all of it. ☐ most of it. ☐ parts of it. |

Mummy has the Last Laugh – 2

1. Use a dictionary to find the meaning of each word.

(a) theatrical	
(b) sarcophagus	
(c) informed	
(d) emerged	
(e) curator	
(f) artefacts	

2. An actor dressed as a fake mummy because _____

_____

_____

3. Why didn't the stunt work out like the others?

_____

_____

4. Look for two clues in the article to find out the date April Fool's Day falls on. Explain each clue.

_____

5. The reporter who wrote the newspaper article interviewed two people and wrote what they said. Name these two people.

6. (a) The caption under the photo is: _____

   (b) Explain why these words were chosen. _____

_____

7. A newspaper headline often catches our attention and also gives some information about the article. Think of another catchy headline.

_____

My learning log	While doing these activities:		
	I found Q _____ easy.	I found Q _____ challenging.	I found Q _____ interesting.

Mummy has the Last Laugh – 3

1. Write the word from the text that is a homophone for each word below.

   (a) dew _____ (b) two _____ (c) there _____

   (d) bean _____ (e) knot _____ (f) wood _____

2. Underline the correct homophone in each sentence.

   (a) The (be / bee) is buzzing around the flowers.

   (b) The building (sight / site) was muddy after the heavy rain.

   (c) I need to (so / sew) the hole in my jumper.

   (d) There is no cotton left on the (reel / real).

3. The word 'sarcophagus' (a stone coffin) comes from two Greek words, 'sarx' meaning 'flesh' and 'phagos' meaning 'eating'. Explain why these meanings suit the word 'sarcophagus'.

   _____

4. (a) Circle the prefix in each word. | undo   unexpected |

   (b) What meaning does the prefix give each root word?

   _____

5. The words 'Egypt' and 'Egyptian' have the /ɪ/ sound spelt with a 'y'.

   (a) Circle the words where the 'y' makes the same sound as in 'Egypt'.

myth	display	gym	pyramid
mummy	scary	yesterday	mystery

   (b) Where is the 'y' in these words? _____

6. In the first paragraph, find the word in which the grapheme 'ch' appears

   twice. _____

   The two 'ch' sounds are different. Use a dictionary to find:

   (a) words with 'ch' like 'school'. _____

   (b) words with 'ch' like 'children'. _____

My learning log	Colour:	I [understand] / [need more practice on] homophones.
		I [know] / [don't know] when to use the prefix 'un-'.
		I [can read] / [am not too sure about] the different 'ch' sounds in words.

Fossil Poetry

Curriculum Links

Activity	Code	Objective	Outcome
Text	C3 C6 C10	• Listen to and discuss a wide range of poetry • Increase their familiarity with a wide range of books • Recognise some different forms of poetry	• Can identify key features of a range of poetry forms
Comprehension	C5 C11 C15 C16	• Use dictionaries to check the meaning of words that they have read • Check that the text makes sense to them, discuss their understanding and explain the meaning of words in context • Identify main ideas drawn from more than one paragraph and summarise these • Identify how language, structure and presentation contributes to meaning	• Can use a dictionary to find and check word meanings • Can summarise the main idea of a poem • Can identify and discuss different forms of poetry
Word Reading	WR1	• Apply their growing knowledge of root words, prefixes and suffixes	• Can identify root words in words with prefixes and suffixes added • Can use the prefix 'un-' to create new words • Can recognise the suffix '-sure'

Additional Teacher Information

Definition of Terms

Poetry
Poetry is a genre which utilises rhythmic patterns of language. The patterns include metre (high-low stressed syllables), syllabification (the number of syllables in each line), rhyme, alliteration or a combination of these. Poems often use figurative language.

Acrostic
An acrostic is a poem based on a keyword. The first letter of each line in the poem is used to make the keyword.

Rhyme
Correspondence of sound between words or the endings of words, especially when these are used at the ends of lines of poetry.

Free verse
Free verse is an open form of poetry which does not use consistent metre patterns, rhyme or any other musical pattern. It often follows the rhythm of natural speech.

Links to other Curriculum Areas

• Science – Rocks: Fossils are formed when things that have lived are trapped within rocks

Terminology for Pupils

poem
rhyme
phrase
sentence
bracket
root word
prefix
synonym
antonym
suffix

Suggested Reading

• Visit <http://www.abc.net.au/beasts/fossilfun/> to read more about how fossils form in different areas.
• *Fossils* (True Books) by **Ann O. Squire**
• *Fossils Tell of Long Ago* (Let's-Read-and-Find-Out Science 2) by **Aliki**

Text

Teacher Information

- This collection of poems includes free verse poems, an acrostic and a rhyming poem. Poem 3 explains the process of forming fossils and Poem 4 gives information about palaeontology and the work of a palaeontologist.
- Pupils will need some knowledge of different poetry forms to fully comprehend the texts.

Introduction

- If available, show pupils a collection of fossils. If none are available, look at photographs of fossils online or in books.
- Discuss the work of a palaeontologist. Ask pupils whether they think this type of work would be interesting, and why.

Development

- Write the following words onto the board: *preserved*, *organisms*, *amber*, *sediment*, *pressure*, *fossils*, *palaeontology*, *palaeontologist*. Discuss the meaning of these words.
- Read and discuss the poems with the pupils. Assist pupils to decode new words if necessary. Question individual pupils to gauge their understanding of what they have listened to or read. Pupils should also ask questions about parts of the poems they are unsure of, in order to improve their understanding of them.

Differentiated Individual/Paired/Group Work

- In groups, share ideas for words that could be used in a descriptive poem about fossils; for example, ancient, sandy, rock hard, dead, bones, shells.
- Pupils should use these words to write a shape poem in the spiral shape of an ammonite fossil (see artwork on page 109).
- More able pupils should be encouraged to have more spirals in their poem than less able pupils.

Review

- Pupils should present their poems neatly and share them with the class.

Comprehension

Teacher Information

- Pupils may need a dictionary to complete questions 5 and 6.

Introduction

- Ask pupils to tell things that they learnt about fossils or palaeontologists as a result of reading the poems.

Development

- Assist pupils to identify features of each poem. Poems 1 and 2 are free verse, Poem 3 is acrostic and Poem 4 is a rhyming poem.
- Remind pupils how to use a dictionary efficiently; i. e. alphabetical order and retrieval by 1st, 2nd and 3rd letters. Give each pupil, or pair of pupils, a dictionary. Write words from the text onto the board for pupils to find.
- Discuss the comprehension activities on page 110, then allow pupils to complete the page independently.

Differentiated Individual/Paired/Group Work

- Pupils write an acrostic poem. Less able pupils could use the word 'fossils' and more able pupils 'palaeontologist'.

Review

- As a class, pupils can share their acrostic poems. Which letters did they find the hardest to use?

Word Reading

Teacher Information

- The activities on page 111 focus on root words, the prefix 'un-', synonyms, antonyms and the ending '-sure'.

Introduction

- Reread the text, but first explain to pupils that the focus will be on words. Whilst reading, ask pupils to circle any words with the prefix 'un-'.

Development

- Look at words with the prefix 'un-'. Discuss how adding this prefix makes the words negative; for example, 'do' becomes 'undo' and 'expected' becomes 'unexpected'. Write sentences containing the pairs of words; for example, Peter was *kind* to Marissa, but *unkind* to me.

- Ensure pupils are familiar with the terms 'synonym' and 'antonym'. Give some examples (happy: synonym is glad, antonym is sad). Elicit some examples from the pupils. Pupils suggest sentences for pairs of synonyms and antonyms, to be written onto the board; for example, happy = glad/sad. Ben was *glad* he had homework, but Krista was *sad*.

- The '-sure' words in question 6 should be spoken out loud, so pupils can hear the specific phonemes focused upon.

- Discuss the word reading activities on page 111, then allow pupils to complete the page independently.

Differentiated Individual/Paired/Group Work

- Pupils should find and list words with the end sounds of '-sure' and '-ture'; for example, measure, treasure, creature, adventure.

- Pupils should write a short story containing some of these words. Less able pupils should try and get six of these words into their story, but more able pupils should be encouraged to use as many words as they are able.

Review

- In groups, read their stories and provide feedback.

- Who managed to include the most '-sure' and '-ture' words in their story?

Assessment

C3	Ask the pupils to state which poem they liked the most and least, and give reasons for their choices.
	They could consider: Which poems did they find easiest and hardest to understand? Do they prefer the formats of certain poems? Did they learn anything from the poems?
C5	Present the following list of words to the pupils and ask them to write them in alphabetical order:
	can, cover, chisel, carefully, clean, clue, claw
WR2	Call out (or write on the board) the following words and have pupils pair the words into synonyms. Then write a sentence containing each pair of synonyms.
	tough, tidy, wreck, stones, nail, tiny, rocks, hard, clean, mend, miniscule, repair, claw, body, destroy, corpse

Answers

Comprehension

1. fossils
2. (a) 4   (b) 1, 2 and 3
3. (a) how fossils are formed
   (b) palaeontology and the work of palaeontologists
4. (a) 4   (b) 1 or 2   (c) 1 or 2   (d) 3
5. (a) preserved   (b) organisms   (c) sediment
6. Frozen in time
7. difficult
8. Answers will vary but may include:
   They are sent to museums and displayed; They are sent to other palaeontologists or scientists for further study etc.
9. pressure, minerals and time

Word Reading

1. fossil
2. (a) remain   (b) preserve   (c) earth
   (d) destroy   (e) label   (f) cover
   (g) careful/care   (h) expose   (i) number
   (j) study   (k) cover   (l) clean
3. (a) unearth, uncovered
   (b) The prefix 'un-' means 'not, reverse action, deprive of, release from'.
      It gives the root word a negative (and sometimes opposite) meaning.
   (c) settle, clean, frozen
4. revealed
5. (a) preserved   (b) dead   (c) frozen
   (d) different   (e) covering   (f) tiny
   (g) ancient   (h) full   (i) clean
6. (a) pressure
   (b) Teacher check; e.g. measure, treasure, pleasure, closure

Fossil Poetry – 1

Read the poems about fossils.

1. Long dead, but still remaining,
   Frozen in time, preserved forever.
   Animals, plants and organisms
   Tell about the past—if only we can unearth them.

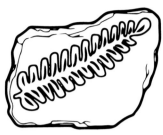

Preserved fern

Petrified wood

2. Fossils
   Dug up
   Past life uncovered
   From rock, soil, amber
   Once hard parts — bones, shells
   Different types preserved in different ways.

3. First a dinosaur dies.
   Over the body, soil, mud or rock stop it from being destroyed.
   Sediment layers build up over time, covering it.
   Soon the layers press down on the remains.
   In tiny spaces of the bones, minerals settle.
   Left in place, pressure, minerals and time turn
   Sediment into rock and bones into fossils.

Dinosaur thigh bone

4. Palaeontology is the study of ancient life.
   Fossils make this study full of strife.
   Plants and animals from the past
   Are uncovered by wind and water and exposed at last.
   Small drills and chisels carefully clean
   Fossils from the rocks so they can be seen.
   Numbered, photographed and labelled too
   Cleaned, repaired and studied in a lab for clues.
   Skeletons, droppings, teeth, nests or claws
   A palaeontologist solves the puzzle of life that once was.

Ammonite fossil

My learning log	When I read these poems, I could read: ☐ all of them. ☐ most of them. ☐ parts of them.

Fossil Poetry – 2

1. The topic of all the poems is _____.

2. (a) Which poem rhymes? Poem _____

   (b) Which poems do not rhyme? Poems _____

3. In a phrase or short sentence, write what Poems 3 and 4 are mainly giving information about.

   (a) Poem 3 _____

   (b) Poem 4 _____

4. Write a number from 1 to 4 to tell each type of poem.

   (a) rhyming   Poem ☐   (b) free verse   Poem ☐

   (c) free verse   Poem ☐   (d) acrostic   Poem ☐

5. Write a word from the poem that matches each meaning. The poem in which the word is found is in brackets.

   (a) keep something in its original state (1) _____

   (b) individual animals, plants or single-celled

        life forms (1) _____

   (c) mineral or organic matter deposited

        by water, air or ice (3) _____

6. Which phrase in Poem 1 means
   almost the same as 'preserved'? _____

7. Poem 4 tells that being a palaeontologist is (easy/difficult)

   _____ work.

8. What do you think happens after fossils are studied in a lab?

   _____

9. The three main things that create fossils are _____

   _____.

My learning log	While doing these activities:		
	I found Q _____ easy.	I found Q _____ challenging.	I found Q _____ interesting.

Fossil Poetry – 3

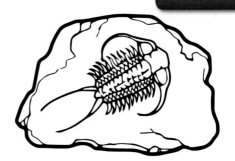

1. Which word comes from the Latin *fossilis*

   meaning 'dug up'? _____

2. Write the root word from which these words were made.

   (a) remaining _____ (b) preserved _____ (c) unearth _____

   (d) destroyed _____ (e) labelled _____ (f) covering _____

   (g) carefully _____ (h) exposed _____ (i) numbered _____

   (j) studied _____ (k) uncovered _____ (l) cleaned _____

3. (a) Underline the prefix in the words 'unearth' and 'uncovered' and circle the root words.

   (b) What does the prefix mean and what does it do to the words?

   _____

   (c) Circle the words that can have this prefix added.

   | time | forever | settle | rock | clean | frozen | past | teeth |

4. Write the word that is a synonym of 'exposed' and could be used in the definition below.

   | revealed | hidden | found |

   An area uncovered by wind and water and _____ at last.

5. Write the word from the text that is an antonym for each word below.

   (a) destroyed _____ (b) alive _____ (c) thawed _____

   (d) same _____ (e) exposing _____ (f) massive _____

   (g) modern _____ (h) empty _____ (i) dirty _____

6. (a) Find a word in the text with the '-sure' ending. _____

   (b) List four other words that end in '-sure'.

   _____   _____   _____   _____

My learning log	*Colour:*	I can recognise / am not too sure about root words.
		I know / don't know when to use the prefix 'un-'.
		I understand / need more practice on synonyms and antonyms.

Types of Rocks

Curriculum Links

Activity	Code	Objective	Outcome
Text	C3 C4 C6	• Listen to and discuss a wide range of non-fiction and reference books • Read books that are structured in different ways and read for a range of purposes • Increase their familiarity with a wide range of books	• Can identify key features of a non-fiction text
Comprehension	C5 C11 C16	• Use dictionaries to check the meaning of words that they have read • Check that the text makes sense to them, discuss their understanding and explain the meaning of words in context • Identify how language, structure and presentation contribute to meaning	• Can use a dictionary to find and check word meanings • Can identify key features of a text presented as a table
Word Reading	WR1 WR2	• Apply their growing knowledge of root words and suffixes • Read further exception words, noting the unusual correspondences between spelling and sound	• Can identify a word's root word and suffix • Can distinguish the spelling of different homophones

Additional Teacher Information

Definition of Terms

Table

A table is a graphic organiser used to record information. The items or criteria are written as a single word, phrase or statement, as headings. Important information is recorded relating to each criterion. Tables allow comparisons to be made.

Hyphen

Hyphens are short strokes (-) used to connect the parts of a compound word or the parts of a word divided for any purpose.

Heading

A heading tells the reader what a section of a text is about. Headings guide the reader through the text by showing the main idea of the texts being read. Headings are usually larger than the body text and are often in bold text.

Links to other Curriculum Areas

• Science – Different kinds of rocks

Terminology for Pupils

table
word
text
hyphen
heading
homophone
sentence
suffix
root word
antonym
synonym

Suggested Reading

• *National Geographic Kids Everything Rocks and Minerals: Dazzling Gems of Photos and Info that will Rock your World* by **Steve Tomecek**

• *Rocks: Hard, Soft, Smooth and Rough* (Amazing Science) by **Natalie M. Rosinsky**

• *The Rock Factory: The Story About the Rock Cycle* (Science Works) by **Jacqui Bailey**

• *If You Find a Rock* by **Peggy Christian** (a book in poetry form about the joys of discovering and using rocks)

Text

Teacher Information

- The most commonly known rocks for each category are provided as examples. Keen pupils may know of others (or wish to research other rocks).

Introduction

- If available, show pupils examples of the three types of rocks. Let them handle the rocks, so they can see any grains, bubbles, layers and lines, and feel how hard or soft they are. If rocks are not available, good quality images from the Internet or books will be needed.
- Pupils could watch many of the videos available online to further understand how different rocks are formed; for example, < https://www.youtube.com/watch?v=sN7AficX9e0>

Development

- Write the following words onto the board: *features, classifications, molten, solidifies, coarse-grained, minerals, cemented, pressure, chemical processes, sculptures*. Discuss the meaning of these words.
- Read and discuss the information in the table with the pupils. Assist pupils to decode new words if necessary. Question individual pupils to gauge their understanding of what they have listened to or read. Pupils should also ask questions about parts of the text they are unsure of, in order to improve their understanding of it.

Differentiated Individual/Paired/Group Work

- Pupils produce a fact sheet or poster about one of the three types of rock. This could contain information from the text on page 115 and other information from books or online. Differentiation would be by outcome, although teachers could stipulate a minimum amount of text to be included by pupils of varying abilities.

Review

- Pupils should share their work in a small group.

Comprehension

Teacher Information

- Pupils may need a dictionary to complete question 4.

Introduction

- Assist pupils to identify features of a table. How is the text presented? Does this make it easier or harder to understand and find information? Why?

Development

- Remind pupils how to use a dictionary efficiently; i.e. alphabetical order and retrieval by 1st, 2nd and 3rd letters. Give each pupil, or pair of pupils, a dictionary. Write words from the text onto the board for pupils to find.
- Pupils should give a summary of each rock type using their own words.
- Discuss the comprehension activities on page 116, then allow pupils to complete the page independently.

Differentiated Individual/Paired/Group Work

- Pupils should list what different rock types are used for and why; for example, Kitchen counters are made from igneous rocks because they are hard and glassy.
- Less able pupils should give one use and reason for use for each rock type, whilst more able pupils should provide three uses and their reasons per rock type.

Review

- As a class, share their lists of uses for the rocks. Which rock type did they find the most uses for?

Word Reading

Teacher Information

- The activities on page 117 focus on homophones, root words, suffixes, synonyms and antonyms.

Introduction

- Reread the text, but first explain to pupils that the focus will be on words. As they reread, ask them to circle any compound words containing the word 'stone' (gravestones, sandstone, limestone). Ask them to give a definition for each of these words. Can they think of any other compound words containing the word 'stone'?

Development

- Ensure pupils are familiar with the term 'homophone'. Give some examples (see/sea; there/their; maid/made). Elicit some examples from the pupils. Pupils suggest sentences for pairs of homophones, to be written onto the board; for example, *son/ sun* = My parents have a <u>son</u> and a daughter./Planet Earth orbits around the <u>sun</u>.

- Some of the antonyms in question 5 include prefixes that give the word an opposite meaning; for example, unpolished and disappear. This is an easy way for pupils to make antonyms of some words. The prefix 'mis-' also gives opposite meanings to words. Think of some words starting with these prefixes, list them on the board, and give their antonyms; i.e. the word without the prefix.

- Demonstrate how to use a thesaurus to find synonyms. Practise finding synonyms for different words with the class, especially for words like 'nice' and 'said' that tend to be overused.

- Discuss the word reading activities on page 117, then allow pupils to complete the page independently.

Differentiated Individual/Paired/Group Work

- Provide pupils with a list of words. They should use a thesaurus to find and list synonyms for these words.

- Suitable words include: nice, said, happy, sad, rich, clever, hot, strong, pretty, fast.

- More able pupils could be provided with a longer list of words to find synonyms for. Or less able pupils could be asked to find three synonyms for each word, and more able pupils at least six per word.

Review

- As a class, compare pupils' lists of synonyms. Which word did they find the most synonyms for? Discuss how using a thesaurus to find synonyms can help to improve their writing.

Assessment

C4	Ask the pupils to choose one of the rock types. They should use the information in the table to write, in their own words, three paragraphs about their chosen rock.
C11	For each rock type, pupils should write a short paragraph explaining one way it is used and why they think the rock is suitable for this use. For example, igneous rocks are used for kitchen counter tops because they are hard and shiny.
WR1	Present the following words to the pupils and ask them to write down the root words: formed, volcanic, cemented, solidifies, processes, buried, depending, folded, horizontal, making

Answers

Comprehension

1. igneous, metamorphic
2. (a) volcanic   (b) layered   (c) changed
3. How they are formed
4. (a) classifications   (b) solidifies
5. (a) Answers may include: the patterns of twists, swirls and folds may look good on a sculpture; easy to sculpt etc.
   (b) Answers may include: it is hard so hot objects won't burn it and sharp objects like knives won't scratch it (hard and dense) etc.
6. sedimentary
7. coarse-grained, fine-grained
8. Answers may include: headings group similar information and ideas; information is easier to read and understand if grouped and written in short points.
9. granite and marble

Word Reading

1. (a) main   (b) be
   (c) where   (d) coarse
2. Teacher check
3. igneous
4. (a) (flow)s   (b) (depend)ing
   (c) (cement)ed   (d) (fold)ed
5. (a) vertical   (b) unpolished, dull
   (c) disappear   (d) below
6. (a) warmth   (b) thick
   (c) middle   (d) powerful

Types of Rocks – 1

Read the information in the table.

Each rock is different. Each has features that tell how it was formed. There are three main classifications of rocks—igneous, sedimentary and metamorphic.

	IGNEOUS (volcanic)	**SEDIMENTARY** (layered)	**METAMORPHIC** (changed)
How they are formed	Molten rock (magma) from the centre of the earth flows to the earth's surface when volcanoes erupt. It cools and solidifies forming rock.	Sediment (bits of rock, minerals, or animal and plant matter) gathers together and builds up to form rocks at the surface of the earth in water or on land.	Heat, pressure and chemical processes change igneous and sedimentary rocks buried deep beneath the earth's surface.
What they look like	coarse-grained (large crystals) or fine-grained, glassy (small crystals) depending on where the rock solidifies—below, on or above the earth's surface; may have air bubbles; hard and dense	rounded grains cemented together in layers; may contain fossils, have wavy, horizontal lines or be dusty	strong bands of different minerals; may appear twisted, folded or swirled
How they are used	gravestones and polished counter tops (granite)	building (sandstone and limestone); paint making, brick making, roads (shale)	roofing, garden stone (slate), building, sculptures, soaps (marble)
Examples	obsidian, granite, basalt	conglomerate, sandstone, shale, rock salt, limestone, coal	slate, marble, quartzite

| **My learning log** | When I read this table, I could read: | ☐ all of it. | ☐ most of it. | ☐ parts of it. |

Types of Rocks – 2

1. Which two groups of rocks can form below the earth's surface?

   _____

2. Write one word from the table to describe each group of rocks.

   (a) igneous _____   (b) sedimentary _____

   (c) metamorphic _____

3. Under which heading would you find the place on the earth where each type of rock forms?

   Obsidian

   _____

4. Which word from the text means:

   (a) groupings or classes?

   (b) make or become hard or solid?

5. Give one reason why:

   (a) marble is used for sculptures. _____

   _____

   (b) granite is used for counter tops. _____

   _____

6. Which type of rocks may contain fossils?

7. Which two words with hyphens describe the crystals in igneous rocks?

   _____

8. Why has the writer presented the text in a table with headings?

   _____

   _____

9. Write two types of rocks someone would choose to use to construct a gravestone with a statue on top.

My learning log	While doing these activities:		
	I found Q _____ easy.	I found Q _____ challenging.	I found Q _____ interesting.

Types of Rocks – 3

1. Circle the word used in the text in each pair of homophones.

   (a) main, mane   (b) be, bee   (c) wear, where   (d) coarse, course

2. Write each homophone in a sentence.

   (a) wear _____

       where _____

   (b) coarse _____

       course _____

   (c) main _____

       mane _____

3. Which word for one of the three types of rocks comes

   from the Latin word 'ignis' meaning 'fire'? _____

4. Underline the suffix and circle the root word in each verb.

   (a) flows   (b) depending   (c) cemented   (d) folded

5. Match the antonyms to the correct words from the text.

   (a) horizontal   *   * unpolished, dull

   (b) polished   *   * vertical

   (c) appear   *   * below

   (d) above   *   * disappear

6. Match the synonyms to the correct words from the text.

   (a) heat   *   * powerful

   (b) dense   *   * middle

   (c) centre   *   * warmth

   (d) strong   *   * thick

My learning log	*Colour:*	I [understand] / [need more practice on] homophones.
		I [know] / [don't know] which parts of words are suffixes and roots.
		I [can recognise] / [am not too sure about] synonyms and antonyms.

Read the email.

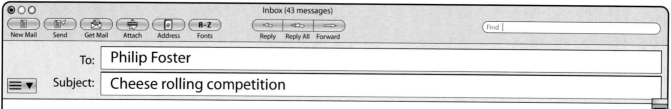

Inbox (43 messages)

New Mail Send Get Mail Attach Address Fonts Reply Reply All Forward

Find |

To: Philip Foster

Subject: Cheese rolling competition

Hi Philip

We're having a great time in England, staying in the town of Gloucester in the south-west. I have to tell you what we did yesterday. We went to a place called Cooper's Hill, not far from here, to see a really unusual competition. You would have loved it!

Can you imagine groups of people chasing a big lump of cheese down a very steep hill? Well, believe it or not, that's what we saw at Cooper's Hill!

The area is famous for its cheese. In May each year, there is a contest called 'The Cooper's Hill Cheese Rolling and Wake'. A large, round, covered cheese is rolled down the steep slope of the hill and chased by a group of runners, or should I say 'tumblers'!

We did not see anyone get to the bottom of the hill by staying on their feet the whole way. Most people slid down, bouncing up and down, rolling over and over or doing cartwheels through the air!

Someone explained to us that the aim of the contest is to try to catch the cheese. But it's heavy and rolls fast and reaches the bottom first. The winner is the first person to reach the bottom and the prize is—the cheese!

There were several races for men and a women's race. There was also one for children. The children's one is uphill not downhill, because it's safer.

Although it is funny to watch, we saw several people get hurt, which wasn't fun. There were ambulances waiting at the bottom of the hill to treat the people who had cuts, sprained ankles or who had hit their head and got a concussion. A couple of people even broke bones. Ouch!

Hope you like the photograph I attached to this email. I think it's funny that all the people in the race have their mouths open, don't you?

See you soon

Your cousin Harry

Catch that Cheese!

1. (a) How is the winner of the race decided?

    _____

    ☐ 1 mark

   (b) What is the prize? _____

2. List things that Harry liked and disliked about the cheese rolling contest.

    ☐ 2 marks

Liked	Disliked

3. Use a dictionary to write the meaning of these words.

    ☐ 2 marks

   (a) concussion _____

   (b) contest _____

4. Write **Fact** or **Opinion**.

    ☐ 1 mark

   (a) Gloucester is in England.   _____

   (b) The children's race is uphill.   _____

   (c) The race is funny to watch.   _____

5. What is the main idea of the seventh paragraph?

    ☐ 2 marks

    _____

    _____

6. Why might all the people in the photograph have their mouths open?

    ☐ 2 marks

    _____

    _____

Total for this page	/10

Catch that Cheese!

1. Tick the word made from each root word in the text.

1 mark

    (a) compete   competition ☐   competing ☐

    (b) bounce   bouncer ☐   bouncing ☐

2. Circle the suffix in this word.   **concussion**

1 mark

3. Write the only word from the first paragraph which has a prefix.

1 mark

_____

4. Find a word in the text that is a homophone for each word.

Write a sentence for each of the four words.

2 marks

    (a) grate   _____

    _____ _____

    (b) hole   _____

    _____ _____

5. Match the synonyms to the correct word from the text.

2 marks

    (a) ajar   •   • aim

    (b) amusing   •   • hurt

    (c) objective •   • open

    (d) injured   •   • funny

6. In the last paragraph, the prefixes 'un-' and 'dis-' can be added on to one word. What is this word?

2 marks

_____

7. Find the word in the email that has 'fame' as its root word.

1 mark

_____

Total for this page	/10	Total for this assessment	/20

Catch that Cheese!

Genre: Informal email

Breakdown of question type/content and mark allocation					
Comprehension			**Word Reading**		
Q 1. Finding information		1 mark	**Q 1.** Root words		1 mark
Q 2. Concluding		2 marks	**Q 2.** Suffix '-ion'		1 mark
Q 3. Understanding words		2 marks	**Q 3.** Prefix 'un-'		1 mark
Q 4. Recognising facts and opinions		1 mark	**Q 4.** Homophones		2 marks
Q 5. Identifying the main idea		2 marks	**Q 5.** Word meanings (synonyms)		2 marks
Q 6. Inferring		2 marks	**Q 6.** Prefixes 'un-' and 'dis-'		2 marks
			Q 7. Root words		1 mark
Sub-total			Sub-total		
			Record the pupil's total result for this assessment.		

Assessment Answers

Assessment – Catch that Cheese!

Comprehension ....*Page 119*

1. (a) The winner is the first person to reach the bottom of the hill.
   (b) The cheese

2.

Liked	Disliked
• Unusual competition	• People got hurt and even broke bones
• Funny to watch	

3. Answers will vary; for example:
   (a) concussion: Temporary unconsciousness or confusion and other symptoms caused by a blow to the head.
   (b) contest: An event in which people compete to win in a sport or other activity.

4. (a) Fact   (b) Fact   (c) Opinion

5. Answers will vary; for example: Some of the competitors got hurt and had to have first aid.

6. Answers will vary; for example: They were shouting, screaming or laughing.

Word Reading..*Page 120*

1. (a) competition   (b) bouncing

2. -ion

3. unusual

4. (a) great, Teacher check sentences.
   (b) whole, Teacher check sentences.

5. (a) ajar, open   (b) amusing, funny
   (c) objective, aim   (d) injured, hurt

6. like

7. famous